The
LOST DAYS
of
AGATHA CHRISTIE

The
LOST DAYS
of
AGATHA CHRISTIE

A Psychological Mystery

Carole Owens

With permission of the *New York Times*, the quote on
the back cover is taken from "A Victorian Spa Marches
On" by Robert Barnard, *New York Times*, Magazine Two,
The Sophisticated Traveler, March 5, 1995.

ISBN 0-918343-03-8
Library of Congress Catalog Card Number: 94-12045

Published by:
Cottage Press, Inc.
P. O. Box 1207
Stockbridge, Massachusetts 01262

For my son Todd

Foreword

In a distinguished career that spanned almost sixty years, Dame Agatha wrote more than sixty-five mystery books and plays. She also wrote two autobiographies. Yet the undisputed Queen of Mysteries left one unsolved: her own.

If a mystery book is a who-done-it, perhaps therapy is a what-done-it. Both detective fiction writers and therapists delve into and solve the mysteries of human behavior. Real or imagined, we want all our mysteries solved.

I too wanted the last of Dame Agatha's mysteries solved. After years of hearing about the mystery of the lost days, I decided to have a try at solving it. Whether it was amnesia or shammed amnesia to hide another truth, it was essentially a psychological mystery. I decided to take Agatha Christie on as a patient and diagnose her problem.

I had the credentials. I was professionally qualified and licensed to render a diagnosis. Of course, there was a problem. My imagined patient, Dame Agatha, was dead. From experience, I could imagine the process if Agatha Christie were in my therapy room, but could I imagine the content? The currency of exchange in therapy is words. I had all her words in fiction and autobiography. The events of Agatha Christie's life used in *The Lost Days* are as she described them in her autobiographies. The point of departure from truth to imagination is a paragraph from Janet Morgan's authorized biography, *Agatha Christie*:

For many years Agatha was worried by her failure completely to reconstruct the events of that dreadful time. After the War she visited the Regius Professor of Pastoral Theology at Oxford, a well known psychoanalyst, who did not practice professionally, but regarded it as part of his University duties to help people who approached him voluntarily. He is said to have told Agatha that her experience had been extremely serious and, *though he was unable to help her replace those missing hours* [stress added], he tried to help her overcome her self-reproach.

The Lost Days begins where the authorized biography leaves off. In this book, Agatha is referred by the Regius Professor to his student, an American psychoanalyst, who helps her reconstruct the lost days and reclaim her memory. It represents a posthumous diagnosis of Agatha Clarissa Miller Christie Mallowan and a solution to the mystery of her lost days. Yet, no matter how diligently I worked to depict the therapeutic process accurately, no matter how much the book may interest people because of the mysteries of therapy as well as the mystery of the lost days, no matter how faithfully I used Agatha Christie's own memories of her life, the solution is, as it must be, a work of fiction.

Carole Owens
Stockbridge
Berkshire County
1995

Contents

Characters

The Patient
    Agatha Clarissa Miller Christie Mallowan   aged 56
    Agatha Clarissa Miller   aged 5
    Agatha Clarissa Miller   aged 12
    Agatha Christie Mallowan   aged 36
Agatha's Family
    Frederick Miller   father
    Clara Miller   mother
    Margaret "Madge" Miller Watts   sister
    Louis Montant "Monty" Miller   brother
    "Nursie"   nanny
    Col. Archibald "Archie" Christie   first husband
    Campbell Christie   brother-in-law
    Max Mallowan   second husband
The Analyst   aged 85
    aged 35

The Analyst's students
The Gun Man

1

The Storyteller

In this large paneled room beneath the brass chandeliers, they have eaten their lunch, chattering and laughing. Now they are quiet, turning their attention to the stage. It is dark with a soft light over the podium. The light picks up the crest of the university emblazoned prominently on the podium. An elderly man approaches center stage. He is tall, thin, stooped, and his clothes hang around his frame. He is unprepossessing, and yet there is a light in his eye, a smile playing at the corner of his mouth, that makes the discerning pause lest they underestimate him. He begins to speak.

"Mr. Chairman, colleagues, students, ladies and gentlemen, it is with pleasure that I address you at this the annual luncheon of our Psychiatry Department. With pleasure, and some surprise. As you know, the annual speaker is carefully selected from among our ranks as an expert, a psychiatrist who has distinguished himself. While I, I will retire this year from a rather indifferent career. So why was I selected? Perhaps it would have been an embarrassment to the department to have kept me around so long without once justifying that decision with some small honor, or perhaps if one lives as long as I have within the confines of a single profession, eventually, one's colleagues honor survival itself."

A shuffle-murmur runs through the audience. It is an inarticulate noise yet universally understood to mean an audience is uncomfortable. The elderly man is alert to re-actions among his listeners, and raises both hands.

"No, no, be calm. No need to fear an hour's apologia. I have been asked to speak on the subject of reclaimed memory, and honesty about oneself is the prerequisite of memory retention or reclamation. If I had lulled myself into the fantasy that I had had a distinguished career, rather than just a long one, I would not remember with absolute clarity the one shining moment, the one great success, in my career. It was a case in which I assisted a woman to recover her memory, and not just any woman. For those much younger than I, in fact for most of you, I will set the stage."

He peers about the room to be sure he has the audi-ence's full attention. He possesses the true grace of old age, patience. The second hand sweeps on the wall clock. Satis-fied, he continues.

"In 1926, the author, Agatha Christie, disappeared from her home in Berkshire, England. Her car was found abandoned at the side of a road in Surrey. The road was lit-tle more than a lane, and at a point where it both de-scended and curved, her car had gone off the track and rested against a tree. It was the first week in December; yet, when she left the car, her fur coat, purse, and case re-mained. Almost simultaneously, she was reported missing from her home in one police jurisdiction, and her aban-doned car was found some miles away in a different juris-diction.

"By 1926, *The Mysterious Affair at Styles* and *The Mur-*

der of *Roger Ackroyd* had been published and were extraordinary successes. Her fame and popularity combined with the mysterious disappearance occasioned a national frenzy of police activity and international newspaper coverage.

"In the first hours, accident or suicide was feared. At one point, 15,000 volunteers were in the fields near the abandoned car searching for clues. When no body and no clues were found, it was postulated that she had been kidnapped. When no demand for ransom arrived, it was suggested that the foul men who acted for profit had bungled the thing and murdered her inadvertently. Finally, her husband Archie was suspected of deliberate murder to gain his freedom in order to marry one Nancy Neele. After a week, the concerned were joined by the cynics, who wrote that Mrs. Christie was in hiding voluntarily for the purpose of promoting her book sales or punishing her errant husband. After eleven days, Agatha Christie was found sitting in the lobby of the Hydropathic Hotel at Harrogate. She had arrived in the approved fashion by train from London. Only one statement was given to the press: *Mrs. Christie has suffered from amnesia*. No questions were entertained. The world balked. Amnesia indeed. No one was satisfied."

He pauses, remembering.

"Twenty years later, I was an American doctor at Oxford, a student of the Regius Professor. I was a generalist seeking a specialty, an iconoclast in a tender young field clinging for justification to absolutes, an atheist in a science taught by demanding that students make themselves over in the image of the god, Freud. The archaic term *alienist*, rather than the term *psychiatrist*, fit me well. I was a trial to my teachers and, in truth, to myself.

5

"It was then that Agatha Christie approached the Regius Professor for help. She wanted to reclaim her memory of those lost days, twenty years ago. The Regius Professor said he could not help her reclaim her memory, but he could help her deal with the guilt."

A student in the audience, with cheerful disrespect for the Analyst, shoots up her hand, waves it impatiently, and speaks all at the same time.

"Professor, what guilt?"

"Ahhh." The Analyst pulls at his ear, an indication that he is thinking. "To understand that, one would first have to understand a woman born in 1890 in England. Agatha Christie, by 1946 Agatha Christie Mallowan, was a Victorian lady. There was the guilt she knew, that is, the guilt stemming from having made a fuss. One did not make a fuss if one was a Victorian lady, and she had made a fuss national in scope. There was the guilt of a lady who had made a public spectacle of herself. The shame of a shy person whose private life was utterly exposed. And there was the guilt, perhaps today we would call it free floating anxiety, about things of which she knew nothing. What had she done in those lost days? Why had she left her home in the middle of the night? Why had she taken on another woman's name when she registered at the Harrogate Hotel, and why was it the name of her husband's mistress? Why couldn't she remember? In short, what had she done, that she could not remember, about which she *should* feel guilt? For this reason, she turned down the Regius Professor's help, reasoning that she could not be free of guilt until she remembered all she had done. The Regius Professor referred her to me. So the odd man, the searcher who did not accept the traditional confines of psychiatry, the sore trial to the department, who cared only for the recuperation of his patients and little for what was accepted practice, I, for that one moment, became *the* man for the job."

The Analyst gives a quick shake to his head and smiles. In that smile, for all the sag of age, one sees a youthfulness.

"You have perhaps heard of my other little successes? In conjunction with the police? Perhaps not. I am apt to use unapproved methods. My little accomplishments are rather hard to place in the context of this sober field. No matter," he waves away other accomplishments, "this case was my first and best."

He stands absolutely still, remembering.

"I met her on a rainy Monday in 1946. We met for one afternoon only. It is all she would allow me. I was in my thirties. She was in her fifties. For twenty years, she had searched quietly, but diligently for help in reclaiming her memory of the lost days. And so our duel began."

The annual lecture is sacrosanct, but this speaker is familiar to the students in the audience. He is their professor; they are his students. The formalities are forgotten.

A second student rises to comment, "I can't see why you say duel as if it were a battle. I mean she wanted to remember, you wanted to help her . . ."

The Analyst regards the student for a minute, then, "You touch the heart of therapy with your question. It is always a battle. Every patient comes and asks politely for help and offers money for your expertise. You sit, passive, available, as if to say, I am at your disposal. Wasted words

7

on wasted paper claim a good therapist can avoid patient resistance. Good trees died in aid of that fantasy. Every patient resists. It is ambivalence itself that motivates the first appointment. The patient wants to do something and can not, or wants to stop doing something and can not. In the asking for help, the desire and resistance are there in equal measure, or the patient would not need you. When Agatha Christie entered my office that rainy day, she was there, her memory was there, and *the reason to resist remembering* was there. Otherwise, Agatha Christie would simply have remembered years ago without help. You will have to expect the resistance and expect that after a time, the balance of labor must shift and it will be the patient who sits passively and accepts the insights of the therapist."

The pattern is set; the lecture has become a dialogue.

A third student, more strident, rises. "Right, or admits it was all a hoax. Amnesia, that is the stuff," he looks around tipping his fellow students that he is about to make a joke, "the stuff Agatha Christie books are made of." His reward is a general titter.

The Analyst waits a respectable time, and asks, "Is amnesia so melodramatic an occurrence?" When no answer comes, he continues. "People can lose and regain memory."

The curious student, the first to rise and ask a question, now has another. "You mean spontaneous reclamation of early memories? All at once, forty years later, you're pouring a cup of coffee or something, and you remember your father sexually abused you? That happens?"

The Analyst says simply, "Yes."

It is now a dialogue spreading through the room. First one student and then another joins in.

"Well, if you believe it happens, I mean, *how* does it happen? Doesn't something have to trigger it? I mean, it seems so hard to accept."

"Yet it has happened to you," the Analyst says.

"Me?"

"All of us. Reification: the experience of one of the five senses triggering an intact detailed memory long forgotten. You pass a bakery and smell rhubarb pie. A smell you have not experienced since childhood and a detailed picture of your grandmother's kitchen is reclaimed. Drug-induced memory loss is regained by the passage of time, healing, and the decrease of the drug in the system. I was given Valium intravenously to aid in a rather unpleasant medical procedure. The result was absolute loss of memory of the 45-minute medical procedure. Several weeks later, when my health was fully regained, I all at once remembered the procedure in detail: the physical details of the operating room, conversation between doctor and nurse, even the physical sensation of the procedure. There are three major causes for memory loss: self-imposed, drug-induced, inducement by physical or psychological trauma. Self-imposed memory loss is accomplished," the Analyst nods at a student shaking his head, "yes accomplished, to make room for more immediate needs and to protect oneself. The details of your grandmother's kitchen is less relevant today than the details of your thesis, so you file the less relevant information away. Or you forget in order to protect yourself. I feared the medical procedure intensely

9

and only remembered it when I was strong enough to do so, and it was safely over."

"Right! Self-imposed. A hoax!" a student in the rear shouts out.

Another student says, "Shush, Randy," and turns her attention to the podium. "So you think the psychiatrist I read about being sued for *inducing* memories in patients is innocent; the patient really remembered early abuse by her father."

"I think there is a great deal of difference between truth in the therapy room and fact in the courtroom," the Analyst begins his answer, and stops. He begins again. "Agatha Christie came to me for help in 1946. She wrote two autobiographies after that and never mentioned what happened in the lost days nor did she mention our meeting. A woman with a meteoric career with a single lapse and I, a man with an indifferent career and a single victory, sat together in 1946. What is fact? Not truth, fact? Fact is that Agatha Christie lived a successful life solving fictional mysteries and died leaving the world in ignorance about one real mystery in her life. So my answer to your question is that we live in a world where we have come to believe truth is found in the courtroom and truth is not even sought there, only fact. In that context we, the psychiatrists, any scientists, can learn nothing. In the world of fact, that which is supported by evidence, the afternoon session between Agatha Christie and myself never happened."

Hands go up all over the room, waving with simultaneous bursts of speech from every corner. "So are you going to tell us? Did she finally remember? *What* couldn't she remember? Was her guilt justified? Had she done something terrible?"

The Analyst seems slightly surprised. "So, without evidentiary proof, you believe me?"

"Did she reclaim her memory of the lost days?"

"She did." The Analyst is nodding.

"So you *know* what happened?"

"Yes." Still nodding.

There is another burst of simultaneous questions. "But how did you do it if she resisted remembering for twenty years? What did you do that other doctors hadn't? Was it genuine amnesia, or was she covering up? What happened in the lost days? Will you tell us?"

"Yes, I will tell you. I may because Agatha Christie gave me permission to do so if I would wait until after her death." Then the Analyst adds, quietly, "I will answer all your questions, but I will not ask you to believe. You are the children of today."

All pretense at formal lecture falls away. The students are crowding forward, sitting in a tight knot under the podium. It is story hour and all eyes are wide and fixed on the storyteller.

2

The Introduction

*Introducing two people is not
enough to form a relationship.
A third element is necessary:
a mutually agreed upon task.
A stool needs three legs to stand.*

By 1946, I had a consultation room in London. It had all the pieces of my profession. There was the analyst's couch. There were big cushy leather chairs. A large mahogany desk sat in front of the window. On the desk, tables, and floor were colored glass-shaded lamps to mellow the light in the room. There were books, patient files, academic papers, but I am afraid they were all atumble on every surface, even on the analyst's couch. I was like my consulting room. All the pieces of professionalism present but awry. I sought to attain the neutral professional tone typical of a clinician and the cool clinical presence I had been taught, and probably failed. I was young, thirty-five; younger still in experience. I had an idea the room was perfect as it was, to give the impression to a client that he could take off his shoes, light his pipe, and tell me all. I wonder what impression it really gave.

It was a rainy Monday. The rain outside the window and the lighting enhanced, I hoped, the aura of warmth, comfort, and intimacy inside. The woman was in her fifties. Her demeanor was in sharp contrast with the room. She sat in a chair, neat and rigid. She was well dressed, and was, in some indefinable way, *somebody*. She had a look of anticipation whether of something positive or negative, I did not know.

I was, I think, deferential to my new patient. I was, I know, excited about the case.

I sat in a chair in front of my desk, not behind it, because I believed the desk was a barrier. A physical barrier, certainly, but also as a symbol of importance, the desk separated me from my patient hierarchically. I remember my first words were about the Regius Professor.

"When the Regius Professor at Oxford first mentioned your case to me, he used the name Mrs. Max Mallowan."

She did not answer me.

"I didn't realize, therefore, who you *were*." I reached behind, and pulled her file out of the heap on the desk. "Then he sent your file."

Although she ignored what I had said, she spoke for the first time. "How did you do that?"

"Do what?"

"Reach into that heap on your desk and effortlessly put your hand on the right file?"

"Some people *need* order. I am tolerant of a little disorder."

"Because you can pull order out of disorder." She was speaking, but not responding to what I said.

I was caught offguard by her. I pulled at my ear, a habit I have when I am thinking, or is it searching for a thought? I tried to return the conversation to the place where I had left it.

"You are Agatha Christie."

"Does it matter so very much?"

"No, of course not. No, wait. Yes, it does. Certainly it does. If you were not who you are the things that happened to you would not have happened to you the way they hap . . ." I was trapped in the midst of my own verbiage with nowhere to go. ". . . pened." I looked at her beseechingly. "You do see that, don't you?"

"Oddly, I do understand you."

I was relieved, and yet this was not a propitious beginning. I retreated behind what today you students call psychobabble.

"Good. Then, Mrs. Mallowan, the purpose in this room is to find out who we are. All parts of ourselves and our lives are important."

"We? Like the hospital nurse, 'how are *we* feeling today after *our* operation'?"

Our eyes met, and I knew posturing was not going to impress her. I had the good grace to laugh. So did she.

I said, "*Not* like the hospital nurse. It is not condescension. I mean it quite literally. I learn about myself, my abilities and shortcomings, as I attempt to help you."

She was still smiling. "Not too many, one hopes."

"Too many?"

"Shortcomings."

"Oh, ah, shortcomings. Well, we can't know . . . yet."

I seemed able to do nothing but amuse her.

She laughed, "It is not true; it can't be! Am I your first patient?"

"'Fraid so. You are my first patient. Well, no, first *psychoanalytic* patient. I have had many other patients, for physical disorders. I was a medical doctor and decided to specialize—general practice in America, and then specialization at Oxford, in England."

"I know where Oxford is."

Of course she did. Now I was silent.

"Well, since I am your first lunatic patient, we can't know you are any good. We must live in hope."

I winced at the word *lunatic* and once more retreated, this time behind my file. I scanned it, appearing to read, though I knew it by heart. "Your goal is to reclaim your memory of the events that happened twenty years ago, in 1926."

She sat in silence. I realized she could not discuss herself. Literally, she had not a word to say. She was animated only if the topic was my poor self. I decided my best course was to make guesses. If I guessed right, she might be surprised into speech. If I guessed wrong, she would certainly correct me.

"Your file has information about the eleven days you disappeared, from December 3 to December 14, 1926, but there is no direct account."

Not a word.

"There are facts about where you went, how and where you were found."

Silence. Nor did she shift position; she sat bolt upright in true Victorian fashion. In her lap, her hands were folded neatly over her purse clasp.

I closed the file and looked at her. "I had the impression when reading this that you may have been told these things by the doctor you saw at the time, by your family, or may have read the news accounts, rather than actually regaining your memory."

She leaned toward me. Her voice was full of warmth, almost like a child's. "Yes. It *was* rather like that. I accepted the account told to me because it *seemed* accurate. Yet I wondered, I really concluded that acceptance was not quite the same as ordinary, as normal, recollection. It is *not* the same, is it?"

"As an adult you are told a story about your baby-hood. The events then *seem* to become part of your memory. In fact, it is the *account* you remember, not the actual events."

She was excited. "Yes. Indeed, yes. And while you have a kind of memory, it is a poor kind. From the external view, as it were."

As quickly as she had changed from stern and silent to excited, she now changed from excitement to a marked defensiveness.

"And then there is what the outsider does not know so could not tell you." Her mouth almost clamped shut. It reminded me of her hands folded over her purse clasp.

I tried again. "The events you want to remember happened twenty years ago. May I ask why you are here now?"

No reply. The silence upset me. I had, in some way, lost ground. I rose, turned away from her, and placed the file back on the desk. It was then that I saw my scrapbook. I reached for it, but only got hold of a corner. As I turned, it fell open on the floor between us.

She looked down. "You made this scrapbook?"

"Yes."

"These newspaper cuttings are twenty years old. Yellowed. Curled where the paste did not hold. You made this scrapbook at the time, in 1926?"

"Yes. I was fifteen."

"I was thirty-six. Married. A mother."

I knelt to pick up my scrapbook. She left her chair,

19

and knelt to help me. We sat on the floor together leafing through.

"You were such a famous writer, your disappearance was front-page news daily." I read some of the headlines aloud. "December 6: Agatha Christie Disappears. December 7, 8, and 9: Search For Christie. December 10: Publicity Theory Scorned. December 12, 13: 15,000 Volunteers To Aid Police In Search. December 14: Agatha Christie Found At Hotel Under Assumed Name. December 15: Her Husband Declared Her Disappearance Due To Loss Of Memory. December 16: Husband Asserts She Still Suffers; Specialists Are Skeptical In Accepting His Statements; Demand For Her Books Jump."

"No one believed me." She said this in a small voice. It was a pained voice, when it might only have been a voice remembering pain. "They believed it was a stunt done for the publicity."

"I was at school. I had just read *The Murder of Roger Ackroyd.* There were daily news accounts even in New York. I read the lengthy opinion pieces about where you had gone and why, or alternately who had killed you and why. Pure guesswork really. Even then I believed it to be an amnesia case."

She pounced on my last words. "Why?" she demanded.

I was determined to maintain a light tone and trap her into conversation of more than a sentence at a time.

"Oh, untutored intuition and the arrogance of youth. The certainty of ignorance. Perhaps a young man who wanted to be a doctor drumming up imaginary business."

"To have been believed, even by a child."

"Not a child; I was fifteen. I thought I'd join the hunt. I would join the thousands who came to search for you, but I would be the one to find you. I had heard something or other about tramp steamers that sounded just the ticket."

Her voice became taut. "But you did not go; you stayed in America, stayed at school?"

I reassured her. "I did not go; I stayed in school."

Whatever spell had been created on the Turkey carpet among the yellowing newsprint was broken. She resumed her chair and the identical pose, rigid back, hands folded over the purse clasp, the mouth clamped shut, as if that posture was "home base" to which she must periodically return.

"Good," she said and was again silent.

I looked at her, and realized in that rigidly correct posture was a wealth of information. It was characteristic of another age, of conventions not confidences, manners not emotions. She was *bolt* upright, hands and mouth *locked*, defended on all sides.

"So now we know why it still plagues you after twenty years—guilt. Embarrassment at a public display, the inconvenience you may have caused others, private grief exposed to public scrutiny. Guilt and shame. The shame that the explanation for your behavior, amnesia, was thought by others to be an inadequate, or possibly a contrived, excuse."

The insight that was a coup for me was obvious to her. She did not move a muscle.

"Sufficient cause. Or, do you disagree?"

I pressed on. "Caught in the light of public scrutiny,

21

you might have reasoned that a medical condition, one over which you had no control, for which you could not be reasonably blamed, was the only out. Twenty years later the guilt could come from your being in possession of all the facts, and finding it hard to continue to lie but impossible to *come clean.*"

She rose. She was not best pleased. "You said a moment ago that you thought at the time I had amnesia. Before that, you said I may not have normal recall to this day, only memory of a story I was told. Now you contradict that. You say I contrived the whole thing. I did not come here to be further ridiculed or to be further confused."

She might have been Queen Victoria stating, "We are not amused."

I smiled. "Well, nothing is the matter with your recent memory. I said all those things."

She was continuing to stand. "The Regius Professor states that total recall is impossible and then refers me to a novice. Why? The energetic young man, the Yank, who can do the difficult task, or the Regius Professor does not believe there is anything to do? So a novice can do no harm?"

I was excited. I hopped up from my chair, and resumed my chair. I saw a path through the Christie maze. "I neither know nor care what the Regius Professor believes."

Of course I had failed utterly to listen to my patient and understand her meaning.

She was still standing, now gathering her things to leave. "Well, so much for honesty in this room. So much for . . ."

I had to stop her. I rose and stood opposite her.

"As for the things I said, I was stating possibilities. Like you do in your books: is it murder, suicide, or natural causes? I ask was it amnesia, feigned amnesia, or no amnesia? I have been guessing." I could think of nothing else to say but, "Won't you help me?"

She stopped gathering; stopped her motion toward the door.

"What a peculiar thing to say. It is I who came to you for help."

I was silent. Would she stay? She did sit, but on the very edge of her chair.

"Can't you understand?" she asked. "It is not that I will not help, it is that I can not. The days are a complete mystery to me. *But then we all are mysteries, even to ourselves, especially to ourselves.*"

"What did you say? No, wait, I recognize it. I have it! Jane Marple, *The Body in the Library.* Yes. I am right, aren't I?"

"No, no, *no!* Not another fan. Not another reader who believes all one's writing is autobiographical."

At least I had made her laugh. I said, "Not so simple, but it all—the way you live, the way you write—all comes from you, from your experiences, your ideas, your ideals, from who you are."

"Precisely, and we both know what the question is, what it has been for twenty years. Who am I? Am I a liar, or a sufferer? And I, for one, do care what people think, what the Regius Professor thinks. What *you* think. Are you here to help me or expose and admonish me? Now will you tell me why he referred me to you?"

Now I had it. The verbal and nonverbal indicators:

she was afraid to speak. Fear lay at the bottom of her resistance and perhaps of her amnesia, fear of being disbelieved. So much as one single word could be disbelieved, therefore she remained silent. What she wanted was an assurance she would be believed; only then could she start to work to regain her memory.

"Look here, what you want me to understand is that you have tried and tried to remember and can not. Right."

She still sat on the edge of her seat; deciding whether to go or stay. She did not want theory. She wanted trust. Oddly, I wanted the same.

"*Please* sit back. Stay." I was beseeching once again and pulling at my ear. She was rigid, looking toward the door. What a picture we made.

"Alright. It is true, the Regius Professor referred you to me because . . ."

"I knew it! No one has ever believed me!"

"*No.* It is like your books, no one knows what to believe. Whether . . ." Oh where in what textbook was this bit: the patient confesses nothing; the doctor confesses all? I took the plunge. "*Whether* you had amnesia or not, the Regius Professor does not believe anything more can be done in either case."

"Just as I said. I am humiliated, disbelieved, fed a psychiatric placebo in the shape of a charming young man without experience who will dispense with me. You even pretend to be a fan to ease the blow. Disgusting."

Any professional mask I may have thought I wore fell away. "No, actually, you are not the one the Regius Professor sees as a trial. I am."

"You?"

"Yes. You are here because I agreed that you be referred to me even though no one believes you can be helped. Whether you are shamming and wasting professional time in aid of I don't know what, or whether you have amnesia about events so many years ago it is simply too late to reclaim them, no conventional intervention meets the case. I do not quite fit the conventional psychiatric mold, and neither does your problem. My professor was delighted to have a place to send you and your problem, whatever he thinks it is, probably because he sees a symmetry in placing the odd problem with the odd doctor. In any case, I could, in his mind, do no harm. I am a trial to my professors, and a fool for volunteering, in their minds."

"Fool enough even to believe me?"

"It is like a mystery book, one of yours. We won't know the truth until we read to the end. I will believe you, and try to help, and to hell with what anyone else thinks. Please sit back. Tell me the facts. Whatever we discover, I will never repeat it to anyone without your full knowledge and explicit permission. Let them all wonder forever. This is for you, not them. *Now*, may we begin in earnest?"

There was, what seemed to me to be, an eternal pause, and then she sat back and put her purse down on the floor beside her.

She gave me a steady, level look. "One thing more before we begin."

I breathed a sigh of relief; she would stay.

"Is it true this is the fulfillment of your fantasy?" she asked.

"I don't quite understand."

25

"When you were a boy, you thought you would find me and help me and now . . ."

"Yes, I suppose . . ." I stopped and laughed. "Well, well, I do have shortcomings, and the first is, so far you have elicited more personal information from me than I have from you, Mrs. Mallowan."

I took out my notebook and hoped she would begin. She did.

"Then in the spirit of fair play, I will tell you about me. The truth is that I remember nothing to this day. I have accepted others' retailing of the facts. I have made up explanations in fiction. I have racked my brain. And yet, for all that, I feel there is something for which I have responsibility. Something over which I had control. At some point I made a decision. What? When? I do not know. The Regius Professor told me he could not help me to remember, but he could help me feel less shame and guilt. I wanted more than that. How can I be expected to feel less guilty if I do not know what it is that I *did*, or why I did it? How could anyone?"

I had a system. I disagreed with the absolute passivity of my colleagues who seemed to take their cue from the physical sciences and research. It had been demonstrated that even the act of observation changed outcomes, and so the analysts sat and listened. They claimed to know and understand and to be waiting for their patients to talk themselves into awareness without interference. I could not see it. First, say even my presence caused change; wasn't that the point of my presence, the point of my patient coming to me? As for the notion that I may know the diagnosis and cure, and only wait for the patient to discover it, that seemed like cat and mouse; not quite nice. I noted almost everything in my book. My notebook was almost a transcript of the session. Certain notes, however, I would put on a clean sheet, rip it off, and put it in my pocket. These were what I deemed "diagnostically significant" points. I believed I had a job to do, a point at which I must contribute. The diagnostically significant points would be my contribution. I put such a note in my pocket for the first time when my patient had said, "but you didn't go; you stayed in school." The second note I put in my pocket was as she had said, "explanations in fiction."

"Thank you," I said. "Now we know where we are. It plagues you still because of embarrassment over the public scandal, shame at your explanation not being believed, and the most fearful, that there was something you did, and still can not remember, about which you feel guilt very deeply. Our efforts have to be directed toward releasing the information from your subconscious. We will find out what you did and why."

"My mind is not a tabula rasa? It is all there somewhere? I am capable of remembering?"

"Capable, probably; afraid, certainly. If we try together, we may succeed. We have two tasks, I think. To learn what you forgot and to learn why you forgot it. On the night of December 3, 1926, did you . . ."

"No! This is too much. I come to you tormented because I can not remember the events of eleven days of my life in December 1926, and your *cure* is to ask me to remember. If I had a cold, would your *medicine* be to ask me to stop sniveling when you know I can not?"

"Point taken."

I sat silently a moment. How do you get at what is forgotten? Then I leaned forward. What professional technique I had left was no more or less than respect for my patient and a desire to be on her side, not in combat.

"Let us agree we want to know but we do not know. Your memories have not been erased, just stored out of reach. You can retrieve them, but it will be a stretch. You may need help. You have had some good reason to hide them from yourself. You both want and do not want to tell yourself what happened. We are the investigators. We are not here to arrogantly assume or to turn away in fear. We are here together to find the truth."

"Arrange the facts in order, so, and use the little grey cells."

"Yes, and be the great detective. We will sneak up on the facts of the lost days rather than go at them headlong."

"It is like writing a book. A thing I can do."

"Yes, but writing *this* book will take more courage than any you have ever written."

"Why?"

"Because you have a very compelling reason *not* to remember. We all forget things every day. We all tell ourselves the story of our own lives, just as you tell stories in books. We shape the material and mold it into some meaning; we leave some out, and make some up, until we can *live with* what has happened to us."

"And everything in the garden is lovely. I am quite normal, one of the great *un*-lunatic. I, and everyone else, have lost memories. You are young, inexperienced, but not stupid."

"Well, that should be a great relief to us both," I said.

"Now tell me about *my* sort of memory loss, the type that does not happen daily."

Nor was she stupid. She nailed every gratuitous comfort I offered. Palliatives would not suffice. Yet I felt I was, perhaps only inch by inch, chipping away at the fear that strangled her memories.

"Amnesia. There are three causes: drug or alcohol induced, physical trauma, and psychogenic."

"Psycho . . . ?"

"Psychogenic: induced by psychological trauma."

"Psychological trauma?"

"Extreme fear."

"I remember nothing like that."

"The first step, then, is to ask whether you were drinking alcohol, heavily, or using illicit or prescribed drugs prior . . ."

"Absolutely not."

"Not. Then one asks if you had a severe injury, preferably to the head."

"One newspaper reported that I had a bump."

"Your car was found against a tree; perhaps you hit your head on the steering wheel. Was the car damaged?"

"The car was not damaged."

"No. Then presumably it wasn't much of a crash, not much force."

With more enthusiasm than before, she said, "Yes, and that would mean the bump was insignificant."

She was warming to the handling of clues. It was not just a skill of hers, but a way to focus on externals and remove her personal thoughts and feelings from consideration.

I grabbed the scrapbook, anxious to pursue a line that interested her and used her skills. "There are no accompanying symptoms of head injury."

I leafed through and found the newspaper article I needed. I read. "Mr. and Mrs. Taylor, owners of the Hydropathic Hotel at Harrogate reported no perplexity or disorientation in Mrs. Christie's behavior, no complaint of pain, nor did Mrs. Christie ask to consult a doctor. She behaved quite normally." I finished reading and looked at her. "Except that you registered at the hotel under a false name."

"So we are left with . . ."

"Psychogenic amnesia," I said. "Something so painful happened that you were compelled to forget. Psychogenic amnesia is often seen as self-protection, even self-healing. You have heard people say, I don't want to think about it. It is too painful to remember. Psychogenic amnesia is putting it out of your mind absolutely. The memory loss is sometimes confined to the specific events of the psychological trauma."

"But I did not know my name. I did not know where I lived. I called myself Theresa Neele 'late of South Africa.' I advertised in *The Times*, for heaven's sake, December 11, 1926: Friends and relatives of Theresa Neele, late of South Africa, please communicate."

She was agitated.

I moved the subject away from her. "I have read of other cases. There was a case study of a young man who went boating with friends. A severe storm came up very suddenly. They were all in mortal danger. In fact, every other member of the boating party died. The young man, the one survivor, was taken to the hospital. He had no memory of events from before they went out in the boat to the moment of 'awaking' in the hospital. One can understand the sudden nightmare of a fun outing turned to tragedy, the guilt about being the sole survivor, the long period of fear for his own life before rescue, the physical exhaustion, all of which led to amnesia."

"Yes, but did he know who he was?"

"Only in time. So did you. In time."

"But when the police brought Archie to the Hydropathic to identify me, eleven days later, I did not know him; I did not know *myself* for who I was, eleven days later."

"You fled from home, made up a new identity, all memory of the old identity gone. Yet you functioned normally; attention and orientation were normal. You ordered breakfast, took the waters, read the paper. You completely erased the past. It is the stuff movies are made of . . ."

She was taut. "And fiction?" The fear of not being believed was triggered again.

"I would guess great stress or overwhelming fear caused it."

She was relieved because my statement sounded like belief in her amnesia.

She said, "Where do we begin?"

"The beginning. Your earliest memory. We will elicit information; you will give me clues. I will work too, help find the significant events and give them meaning. When we arrive in 1926, we will be armed."

"Mysteries and clues and detectives."

"Yes."

"I can do that."

"So it would seem."

"A collaboration. Poirot and Hastings."

"You will not be alone. I will do my best."

"Which am I? Poirot or Hastings?"

"I am willing to play either part as long as we solve the mystery."

"Agreed. And we begin with my earliest memory, I believe you said." She adjusted in her seat as if preparing for a task. Then she was silent for a moment remembering. She said, "I remember the house in which I was born. I remember Ashfield."

3

The Alienist

*One hundred years ago, doctors who
chose a specialty in mental disorders
were called alienists. They were so called
because their patients were considered
alienated from their true natures,
from normal behavior, and from society,
not because they alienated their patients,
however frequently during therapy
they may do so.*

Neither in her books, nor in my office, was her narrative rich in physical detail. She gave no description of Ashfield. The world came to her more through her ear than her eye. I saw her early life because she had the power to dramatize through dialogue. Her words conjured up the Victorian Age in which she and her family acted out their lives at Ashfield. Her psychological orientation was obviously toward people: what they said; how they said it; shades of meaning and variations in tone. She infused her narratives with these.

She said, "We live at Torquay. It is winter, but I, a small child in my nursery, am safe and warm. I feel smug because of that. I believe the house is blessed, and within its walls, nothing bad can happen to me, to any of us. My mother, and her mother, Granny B., are with me in my nursery. My wise and patient nanny, Nursie, must be somewhere on the periphery. We are waiting for my other grandmother, my father's mother, to arrive." Her tone changed from reverie to quick and strident. "My home, Ashfield, was a safe, beautiful place, almost idyllic. My childhood was as every child's should be, snug and loving, full of good food and good fun."

"Fortunate," I said, and thought that her skills and mine may not be too dissimilar. I too listen for shades of meaning, shifts in tone, instances when tone and content conflict. "What happens next?"

"Next? I grow up."

"On that day, what happens next? You wait for your grandmother and . . ."

"We are waiting for my father's mother, as I said."

"And?"

"*And? And*, I suppose she comes." The content was mundane, her tone angry. What was she defending?

"So your first memory is absolutely uneventful. From it I have a picture of a smug, idle, unimaginative person living in an idyllic family." I tried to avoid sarcasm and probably failed. "On which day was it that you turned into the industrious, imaginative, shy, insecure author I have read about?" She was silent, but neither of us looked away. "In short, Mrs. Mallowan, I don't believe you."

"Oh, very well. We wait. Impatient I say, *Soon will we not all be together, Mother? You and I, Granny B. and Grannie?* I am corrected by Mother. *No, dear. Granny B. and Auntie Grannie.*"

"So?" I said.

No response.

"You felt warm and safe, but in a split second, you feel wrong and foolish because you don't even know how to address your own relative."

No response.

"So?"

"It was more," she said softly. "My family somehow shamed. My father was the stepson of my grandmother's sister, so my great-aunt was also my grandmother. It meant my father and mother were seemingly first cousins. The marriage could *appear* improper."

"She was opposed to my marrying Hugo because we were first cousins, I think. She thought the family was so batty already that we would have completely batty children," I quoted.

"My word, you are a wonder! I wrote those words in *Dead Man's Mirror.*" She was impressed.

"Yes, because you believed that is the way some people would view first cousins marrying."

"Yes, and there is more. Mother lived at Auntie Grannie's from the age of nine *with* Father like brother and sister. But they were in no way *blood* relations—neither cousins nor siblings."

"In that split second you learned shame, and the need to hide things."

"From scrutiny. Yes."

"You also found your profession and the key to your craft."

"The key?"

"You realized a situation could *appear* to be one thing, and actually be another."

"Yes, I did, and that is the key to my books?"

"For the reader, yes. The Queen of Mystery, The Great Deceiver, hides all clues in plain sight. The reader is given all the clues, and is still deceived because the clues are not what they seem."

The idea pleased her.

She said, "You are right! Shall I go on to the next memory?"

I nodded.

"It is later. I am five. We are at the outdoor table in the garden at Ashfield. The table is gaily decorated, a-heap with party foods and wrapped gifts. There is a birthday cake with five lit candles. It is my party. I am to make a wish and blow out the candles. I look around the table at my mother, father, Madge, Monty, and Nursie. All the faces were smiling at me, waiting. Of course it is a bad job that Monty is smiling, cheek. I am trying to think of the best wish ever; they are waiting for me to squeeze my eyes shut and blow." She paused and then whispered, "I see The Gun Man! The Gun Man at my birthday table."

I hadn't heard. "What?"

She raised her voice, almost shouting. "The Gun Man! I wake screaming, *The Gun Man!* Nursie runs into the nursery. Nursie can not calm me. You see, it has all been a dream, a bad dream. The party, the birthday cake, the family around the table, The Gun Man, all of it. I want to stop sobbing so Nursie will not wake Mother, but I can not. I hear Nursie saying, *I am sorry, ma'am, to disturb your sleep, but Miss Agatha had one of her dreams again, and I can't do a thing with her.* I can see Nursie at the end of my bed, rocking back and forth, heel to toe, repeating, *As quiet and clever and well behaved a child as ever was all the day long, and then, the terrors in the night.* Nursie clucks her tongue at the shame of it and rocks heel to toe, heel to toe.

"Then my mother is there beside me on my bed. *Now, now, shhh, tell me what the matter is. You must get hold of yourself. Take a deep breath. Nanny, some water. I can not understand you until you are calmer.*

"I tell her I dreamt that at my party table there was a cruel and dangerous person. *You know him by his light, steely blue eyes, and one hand hidden up his sleeve,* I explain. Mother says he does sound scary indeed. I warm to the sympathy and tell her that the hand could pop out of the sleeve at any moment with a gun in it. *He is The Gun Man!*

"Mother tells me he is not real, only a dream. *Why is he so frightening, dear? What do you think he will do?*

"I fall silent then, unable to speak, and mercifully unable to cry anymore. Mother tucks me up and I sleep."

It was so quiet in the room. I wondered for an instant if she were holding her breath.

"It was a recurring nightmare?"

She nodded.

"You always woke screaming?"

"Yes, and was unconsolable for a long time after waking."

"It rises to the level of night terrors. And the dreams recurred . . ."

"On and off until I was twelve."

"Dreams are clinically significant, a recurrent nightmare even more so."

"Even more meaningful?"

"Yes."

"Well, then, what does it mean?"

"What does it mean to you?"

The turning of a question can irritate a patient, but she seemed prepared, almost anxious to answer.

"I had hoped it was like the other memory, that I had put the fearful dream to good use . . . in my work. I do think I did. It is much the same theme. The other experience demonstrated that facts and circumstances may not be what they seem. In my dream, people are not always

39

what they seem." She was indeed pleased, mugged a bit, and tried an American accent, 'Evil lurks in the hearts of men.' I do think I put the childish fear to good use, don't you?"

Something was bothering me. I answered mechanically, "Oh, yes. You made a career of it. The least likely suspect is the villain—more than a million copies sold."

She read my tone. "That is my formula. How many copies do you think I would have sold if the murderer was the *most* likely suspect?"

"What is it you say in detective fiction? The murderer is unmasked? Your first book, *The Mysterious Affair at Styles*, is about Ashfield . . ."

"About a house *like* Ashfield," she corrected. "It is the world I knew."

"And about The Gun Man."

"What?"

"In the book, the accomplice is believed to be a loyal, loving, trusted member of the household. In the final scene, The Gun Man emerges from behind the mask. The child's dream has become the theme of the adult's fiction. Or, The Gun Man can be looked at another way. *Murder in the Vicarage, The Body in the Library,* murder intrudes into a civilized, well-ordered world just as your Gun Man intruded at a gaily decorated birthday table."

"Yes, yes. Something awful thrust into the midst of the mundane. Shock value, the unexpected. Well, well, I did use it. It is another part of my craft."

She was delighted. I was still bothered.

Hamming it up, perhaps making fun of my seriousness, she quoted, "I mean to say, the *difference* between things as they look and things as they are. I mean here at Woolam Chersey, we have apparently a happy, carefree country-house party. But beneath the glittering surface, Jeeves, dark currents are running. A dreadful fate is creeping nearer and nearer."

"Wodehouse," I said, still answering mechanically.

"Yes. So you see, mine is a theme most English. I fastened on to it as did Wodehouse, Hitchcock, many Brits."

I said, "Your early images were powerful and shaped your adult work."

"Just as you expected. The secret of your craft is that early experiences show us how our minds were made, or made up."

"Neat." I was pulling at my ear, and then I knew what bothered me. "Why couldn't you speak?"

"Couldn't speak?"

"To your mother?" I checked my notes. "You said, *I fall silent then; unable to speak.*"

"I am lost."

"Are you? You tie such neat bows. Early shame and confusion, early night terrors, all experienced, evaluated and used. Neat, complete, folded and put in the bureau drawer; no, in the pages of books."

"You think there should be more to it. But is there? I suspect I fell silent and then to sleep because I was exhausted."

"That is one possibility."

"And the other?"

"When there is something we are afraid to say or choose not to say, we fall silent. We can't or won't say the

41

one thing on our minds, and can't think of anything else. It generally prevents us from speaking at all."

She seemed uncomfortable, but she only said, "How interesting." There was silence. Then she added, "Like Edgar Allan Poe. But I can not see what it has to . . ."

"Was there anything else about the dream that you could or would not tell your mother?" Silence. "Or me?"

"I really can think of nothing else. I am really not used to telling my inner thoughts to perfect strangers. I am doing the best I can."

"Of course. You are doing very well." Our words were gentle and polite, but expressed deadlock nonetheless.

"I was just thinking," I attempted, "that we make the simple mistake of thinking dreams are about other people. After all, we *see* other people in our dreams. In fact, we are the only ones actually present in our dreams. We are the authors, and our dreams reflect only our own ideas and feelings. Say I dreamt about another person, and in my dream this other person (X) was very angry at me. I might say I believe X is angry at me because I dreamt it. Upon investigation, it is more likely I dreamt it because I am afraid X is angry at me, or I am angry at X. I am the author of the dream and the idea."

"The Gun Man was a shocking intrusion into a happy family party or the evil being behind the mask of civility. You suspect precisely what? I *desired* an evil being, The Gun Man, to intrude into my family circle? Or, whether or not there was an evil person behind the mask of a loving family member, the importance is that I believed there was?"

"There is another possibility."

"What?"

"You believed you were The Gun Man."

"How dare you!"

"Not that you *were* an evil, dangerous person; only that you feared you might be. *That* was the real night terror."

"Certainly not. Decidedly not. I was a child, an innocent child."

"A child, Agatha Clarissa Miller, born on September 15, 1890. The third and last child of Frederick and Clara Miller. Frederick was forty-four years old; your mother, Clara, was thirty-eight when you were born. Your sister was eleven years your senior. Your brother, nine years older, was already away at school. Ashfield, the Miller home, appeared to be a stable and happy household. Frederick and Clara had a loving relationship, devoted to one another. You did not attend school, or engage in any group activities with other children. You had a nanny who pronounced you the best behaved of charges."

"You know a great deal about me."

"I care a great deal. Is the publicized biography true?"

"True enough."

"You had no peer group. You lived among adults. You could never be superior in a society of adults, never know more, you could hardly compete, you couldn't even keep up, never win. You never gave the orders. While they perceived a child uniquely quiet and compliant, uniquely able to entertain herself, I think it equally likely you were not complying but escaping, slipping into a world of your own making where you had power, called the shots. Your ability to entertain yourself was more necessity than virtue."

"Later, I thought," she paused, "I felt . . . my writing was more necessity than virtue." She looked at me. "How can you know so much about me?"

"The facts are common knowledge about a famous person. The rest you have just told me, and you gave me the interpretation in your dream. You call the recurring terror "The Gun Man." We know The Gun Man is the cause of great fear because of the name you give him and the fear he engendered in you. The Gun Man materializes in the midst of a beloved family gathering, so the clearest message is that, in your opinion, things in the family are not as idyllic as they seem. The simplest question for me to ask is this: Is young Agatha Miller, in her own opinion, not what she seems?"

"The family said I was exceptionally quiet. Mother frequently said, *It's over, we won't talk about that anymore.* She was a Victorian lady. One did not give into that which was unpleasant, nor did one talk about unpleasant things. Of course I was quiet; what else could I be in the circumstance?"

"Quiet and afraid. Afraid it was you who were not what you seemed. That you were not as happy, not as good as you seemed to be."

"I was The Gun Man?"

"I only said The Gun Man was your invention. You may have *feared* your good manners and docility were a mask and the real you would be a disappointment. You may have believed you had *something up your sleeve.* It is an common expression implying someone is a cheater. You succeeded in gaining the good opinion of your family, but you may have thought you tricked them, *pulled the wool over their eyes,* did not deserve their good opinion. Many people, when they succeed, feel that way. The Gun Man may not be a 'who,' he may have been a symbol of that fear. Or, The Gun Man may have been the symbol of something *wrong* you saw in your family or in yourself but could not say except in your dream."

"Perfectly fascinating. Like a conjurer's trick. The rabbit out of the hat, meaning out of a child's nightmare."

"You are angry."

"No, I am not. Impatient. I am simply no closer to 1926."

"We are closer. We have talked about shame and fear. If you can talk about a thing, you don't have to run from it. Now, search your memory for loss, your first loss. When we have the three, we will have, not the facts of 1926, but the proper background, the motivation for your actions."

"Shame and fear and loss form the motivation?"

"Your earliest two memories have elements of shame and fear; they are literally memorable, and possibly controlling, emotions. On December 3, 1926, you ran away in body and mind. For what reason?"

"Because of shame and fear?"

"And loss. You disappeared on the same day your husband left you for another woman."

There was the sharp sound of exhaled breath as if she had been struck.

I pressed on. "Do you deny the feelings?"

"No."

"Then we will benefit from finding, and *talking* about, the first instance of loss as we have found the first instances of fear and shame. Only then will we be armed."

45

"Loss. I am twelve years old, and everything is lost. My father is dead, my amiable, beloved father. I think nothing can be worse than that until the day my mother calls me into the conservatory at Ashfield. My older sister, Madge, is sitting on the arm of Mother's chair.

"Mother is rigid in her chair. She says, *We are not situated quite as I was led, as I thought we would be.* I can not follow her meaning. Situated? Be direct, Mother! Oh, how I want her to be direct, but I can say nothing at all, and she would not directly say the word, money. Money. There is no money! She only says, *It seems there is, after all, very little.*

"Madge says, *Poor Mummy. But how?*

"Mother will not yield to emotion even now. No remonstrations, no recriminations, no tears. *It does not matter how it happened, Madge dear.* Mother says, *It only remains to decide what is to be done.*

"Madge says, *Poor Mummy. Father's death was enough to face at one time, and now this.* I want to shout, has Father left us destitute? I want Madge to stop repeating, *Poor Mummy.*

"Then Mother says the most terrible words. *There is nothing for it. I have thought it all through. The answer, the only answer, is to sell Ashfield.*

"Madge nods and says everything will be fine. She says, *Of course, we will find you and Agatha something really sweet, just smaller, easier to run as well as cheaper.* She is patting Mother's arm when I finally find my voice.

"At last I find my voice only to shout, *No! Never. We can not leave Ashfield. It is our home. We can't! Don't you see? No one can bear to lose everything at once. First Father, then our home? I will not have it! I can not bear it!* I am both pleading and demanding.

"Mother says, *My poor Agatha. I will try. I will think it all through again. Perhaps* . . . The sentence remains unfinished. My mother is too exhausted even to speak. She rises and leaves the conservatory with Madge supporting her. I stand alone, silent. I remember clenching my fists tightly at my sides. Determination, I suppose."

"Your father died when you were only twelve. It was your first loss, devastating loss, but on that occasion, you found your voice. Apt phrase."

She smiled. "Yes, quiet Agatha found her voice."

"Tell me, an usually quiet girl, why did you shout at your mother? Why then?"

"I was calling a halt. A halt to the amount of loss I could tolerate. I could not lose both my father and my home. I could not fight death, but I could fight the sale of my home."

"You were fighting for your life."

"Yes, at least, my *way* of life."

"And did you succeed?"

"I am fifty-six years old, and I still, to this day, own Ashfield."

"A triumph."

"Perhaps."

"Only perhaps?"

"Keeping Ashfield was a burden to my mother, perhaps an unfair burden."

"Do you *know* it was a burden to your mother?"

"We kept Ashfield, but we never spoke of it again. I *think* it was very hard on her, but she never *said* as much."

47

"Your mother chose to 'get on with things' rather than discuss her grief or her burdens."

Agatha nodded.

"Or your grief."

She nodded again.

"I don't know of any way to resolve grief without talking about it. In fact, talking, incessant talking, is the best therapeutic remedy for grief, loss, shock."

"Time," she said.

"With time we can bury feelings deep, but I don't know that we can cast them off. It was a piling on of unhappiness. To a girl of twelve, the combined loss must have seemed like the end of your world."

"Yes. I had to stop it."

"And you did."

"Yes."

"That may be the most important part."

"I don't quite see . . ."

"Willfulness in the aid of self-protection worked. Obedience would not; silence would not; fighting did."

"Yes, but I felt badly about fighting Mother, insisting on my way even if it forced my mother to pay the price."

"You were successful and yet you do not know if it was the best course?"

"Yes, Ashfield was saved, but at a price."

"You can not blame yourself; you felt you were fighting for your existence."

"Still . . ."

"The grief was not resolved."

"I don't quite see the connection."

"Are you certain you are angry at yourself for having to fight to save Ashfield?"

"Who then?"

"Your father, perhaps?"

"Anger? At Father? Nothing of the sort. Oh, what an agreeable man he is!"

"Dickens, yes?"

"Yes, it's Dickens's description of Mr. Peggotty. Mother and I agreed it was also the perfect description of Father. Yet, with time, we got over his death."

"He died and left you and your mother destitute."

"I did not say *destitute*. Reduced circumstances or strapped; strapped meets the case." She was angry. "Is this your idea of being *armed* to face the events of 1926? Drawing a picture of a cowering, shamed child with unresolved grief and a nasty grasping nature who is angry at the dead for dying? Sounds more like *dis*arming."

From experience with her, I knew Agatha would deny her anger if I observed it directly, so I prepared to sneak up on it.

"Your father was such an agreeable man."

"The most agreeable of men."

"Who left you and your mother quite poor and forced you to make difficult decisions."

"We had no idea of the true state of affairs. We had thought . . ."

"Your father was the manager, the safeguarder of the family. But he was not what he seemed?"

"He did his best for us."

"Not what he seemed to be. Like . . ."

"No! Unthinkable."

". . . The Gun Man."

"Stop!" She rose. "This has nothing to do with The Gun Man."

"Where are you going?"

"Away."

"From yourself?"

"Away! From you!"

"And yourself?"

"You see too much."

"We progress."

With contempt she said, "Poirot."

"We now know why you ran away in 1926. At least what *inside* of you caused you to run. We know where you meant to go."

"*We* know? *Where?*"

"Away from yourself."

Throughout the staccato exchange, she was furiously gathering her things. Now she stopped and faced me.

"I registered at the hotel as Theresa Neele; not my name."

"To be someone else."

"To whom such things do *not* happen." She turned toward the door.

"You came here because at least one part of you wants to know and claim all of yourself, disown nothing, even if it is ugly. In this room, you do not have to assert an idyllic childhood without nightmares. Here you can claim all your parts."

Still she moved slowly toward the door.

"Sit!" My tone shocked and arrested her progress. "Tell me, what things?"

50

"I beg your pardon?" she asked without emphasis.

"You said: *to whom such things do not happen.* What things?"

No response, but no movement toward the door either.

I had to find a question she would answer. "How did you meet Archibald Chistie?"

She gave me the same odd look as when she had said, "you see too much," but she answered. "Actually, I was engaged to another man when I met Archie. Archie was dashing; Archie *was* glamour, handsome, amusing, and all that wrapped in his World War I uniform. Archie was in The Flying Corps. The first unit to go to The Front. The war made everything seem so much more romantic, more urgent. I can still see his telegram in my hand. COME SALISBURY IF YOU HOPE TO SEE ME. ARCHIE. I had to go. I was afraid if I did not go, I might never see Archie again."

She came away from the door and paced as she spoke.

"Yes, I can see Mother and me in the conservatory at Ashfield. I am pleading with her to let me go. She says, *Agatha, if you go to this man, Archibald Christie, you will live to regret it.* But in the end she went with me. I married Archie in haste. We had to have a special license to marry without the waiting period. It cost twenty-five pounds." She stopped abruptly.

"What were you thinking?" I asked.

"Just like Granny, Mother's mother. Granny's prophesies were much dreaded. The old dear was never wrong. No one could ever have wheedled my grandmother out of her savings. She would have fixed him with a shrewd eye and remarked later, *I know his kind. Yes, I've known one or two like him. I know what he is after. I think I'll just ask a few friends for tea and mention that a young man like that is in the neighborhood."*

"Miss Marple," I said.

"Not unlikely, but I was thinking of Mother. Her prophecy about Archie was right. Perhaps *you* could be right about one or two things, even when I am sure that I . . . In any case, we married, and then I hardly saw him at all for the next four years. The war kept us apart."

"Were the absences very hard?"

"One could not complain. It was wartime. So many were in the same position." She had resumed pacing.

"Were the absences very hard?"

"I worked at a hospital dispensary, made myself useful."

"Were the absences very hard?"

"I wrote my first book."

"Were . . ."

"Must you go on repeating yourself?"

"As long as you go on avoiding."

Silence.

"The absences were so hard that you escaped into fiction as you did in childhood," I said.

"Then the war was over and Archie was home."

"You were strangers."

"Yes, somehow, we were still apart. Each in our own world. I am sorry, I do not see how we are getting any further ahead."

"Just helping me with background. After all, you ran away from your marital home. Probably everything about your marriage is important."

"I thought you were most concerned with my early development." Her tone was sarcastic.

I ignored the tone and accepted the words at face value. "Your behavior then is a clue to how you would act if the same sort of thing happened again."

"But the same thing did not happen again."

"No?"

"My father died once. Ashfield was saved once and for all. Those things could not happen again."

"Your father only died once; Ashfield was saved once."

"As I said."

"But your father was a loved one, and Ashfield was a home. The two coming at the same time was the threat of a double loss. You had other loved ones, other homes, other double . . ."

"Double losses. Archie and my mother." She said it as if in a shock of recognition and stopped, standing very still.

"Your mother died in 1926?"

"In the summer of 1926."

"You and Colonel Christie were divorced, and he did marry Miss Nancy Neele?"

"Yes." She sat.

"One newspaper report at the time of your disappearance suggested you may have been murdered by your husband so he would be free to marry his mistress. So I assume the affair started before your disappearance."

"He had been seeing Nancy Neele for some months, actually since the summer."

"The summer of '26 when your mother died."

A nod.

"Once again you faced a double loss, this time not the death of your father and the loss of Ashfield, but the death of your mother and the loss of Archie."

Another nod.

"Did you ever forget who you were *before* December 1926?"

"Actually, yes."

"Tell me."

"An overstatement. I forgot my name." She paused and then, "I had to go to Ashfield for the sorting out. Archie did not come with me to the funeral or to Ashfield."

"He should have been with you."

"I could not blame him. He had to work in the city, and just then he was worried about money. We were forced to let our house at Sunningdale. Archie stayed in town at his club, and I went to Ashfield. All the sad duty one must do after a death—sorting out and disposing of a lifetime of accumulation. It was August, so hot. I was too hot and tired to eat or sleep properly. And all the time, Ashfield, dear Ashfield, had become a sad place now that Father and Mother were gone. I felt it would make such a difference as soon as Archie could get away. We were to go on holiday and then I would be alright. If I could get done at Ashfield, and go away with Archie, I could rest."

"He should have been with you."

"He had business in the city; money troubles."

Since she had recognized the power of the same thing happening again, not specifically, but generically, she had been in shock. In that same attitude of shock, she now sank to the floor, and acted out what she was telling me.

"I sit on the floor sorting papers, Mother's little treasures, and Mother's clothing into five big piles. To save for Madge; for Monty; for me; for the Bishop's Appeal; for the dustman."

She appeared to be holding objects aloft above each pile and then placing it on one. Then she stopped, her hand in the air as if confused on which pile some object belonged.

I watched her with some concern. "You were overwhelmed by the loss, and the work. Archie should have been with you."

She sat looking at the imaginary piles. "I can't think anymore which item should go in which pile. Now the dustman has come." She rose and sat in a chair opposite me. "I rise to write a check, and stop. My name. Of course I know my name perfectly well, but what is it?" She looked directly at me and seemed herself again. "It was a moment of panic so sharp I could feel it physically and then, thank God, it came to me and I wrote Agatha Christie with more relief than I can explain. The dustman took the check, and those bundles were gone. I felt exhausted and relieved as if I had accomplished a great deal and all I had done was write my correct name on a check. Imagine!"

"That day at Ashfield was a warning sign. Sadness, fatigue, isolation can combine and make one physically ill."

"I did not know that."

"You should not have been left alone. Archie should have been with you."

"I told you that part. There were money troubles.

Sunningdale was let. Archie had to stay in the city to work."

"Did he?"

"At any rate, he finally comes. I fly to him. I have waited and waited, believing that when Archie comes it will be a relief. Archie comes and there is no relief. We sit at the table in the garden, the same table at which I sat, decorated for my fifth birthday, in The Gun Man dream. Archie and I sit in the sunshine. Archie is tense. At first I do not notice. I am full of dreams of two glorious weeks in Italy alone with Archie. I ask, *Have you the tickets?* He would only say, *Oh yes, well that's all settled. I'll tell you about it later.*"

"But you wanted to hear about it right then, not later."

"Yes! I tell him, *Now, please.* But he will not answer."

"You knew something was wrong."

"*What is the matter, Archie?* He only says, *Oh, nothing in particular.*"

"You did not believe him."

"No. I insist, *There is something.*"

"And so he told you?"

"He answers me finally, *Well I suppose I had better tell you one thing. We—I haven't got any tickets for Italy. I don't feel like going abroad.* It is just as if he has struck me. *Not going?* I say. He says, *No, I tell you, I don't feel like it.* Just like that, as if not feeling like it explained everything."

"You tried to put the best face on it?"

"Yes, it is like groping in the dark. I try to guess, *You want to stay here with me at Ashfield? Well, that might be nice, as long as we are together.* He says, *You don't understand.*"

"That is how you found out about Nancy Neele?"

"So much worse than just leaving me alone, he had been with *her.* All I could think was, Archie, I don't know you; my husband for eleven years and I don't know you."

"Did you fight? Try to contain the loss as you had after your father died?"

"No, not then. Not yet. Wait, be patient, I told myself, ride it out. These things happen, Archie will come back to me."

"If you are quiet, compliant, understanding just like you were as a child."

"I told it to myself like a catechism. Be of goodwill, good cheer, good hope. Mother was gone, not Archie too! Impossible. So I waited and prayed. As it turned out, Archie and I began and ended at Ashfield."

"When obedience did not work; when silence did not; to hold the marriage, stem the loss, you fought with Archie on December 3, 1926, on the same day you ran away."

Her voice rose, clear and demanding. "How do you know that! How! Tell me how you know what happened in the privacy of my home twenty years ago."

"The significance of an early memory is not that it occurred so many years ago, but that you retained it since. Our mind is like a file drawer and we constantly sort out and throw away to make space. We use a simple criterion: we save that which seems to us to be important—to *mean* something. You saved a memory about shame. In your earliest years you learned your two grandmothers were sisters

57

and that implied your parents were first cousins, and if they were blood cousins, their union was taboo. Had you just made a mistake about how to address your grandmother correctly, it would have been trivial and soon forgotten, but the correct answer was not obvious. You may have been the only little girl in all England with an "Auntie Grannie."

"So what?"

"Social correctness was not obvious, it demanded explaining. In a society, your society, where appearance was all, explanations were *bad form*. In fact, you wrote something about that in *Why Didn't They Ask Evans?*"

"I wrote, *Sir Oswald is a great man and a great man knows better than to explain unless an explanation is demanded.* But it was in *The Seven Dials.*"

"Yes, thank you. More importantly, you wrote it. It means the idea was important to you, and seemed compelling enough so that many years later you make the point in a book."

"So you determined that I carry shame about myself, my family, from one memory?"

"No, also from your relief that I had not left school to search for you."

"Oh?"

"Whatever else you fear about those eleven days, you know for a fact you caused a public scandal and if the publicity had led to my actually sacrificing my schooling to seek you out . . ."

"In general, I would have been mortified." With a spark of fun, she added, "In your particular case, I may end by wishing you had chosen another profession."

"Yes, you well might before the day is over. I hope not."

"But the fight with Archie, how could you know?"

"I could guess about the fight because I could guess you would act the same as you had before. You fought with your mother to save Ashfield, prevent a double loss. Under similar circumstances, you would stop complying and standing silent and fight with Archie to save the marriage: stem the loss and shame of unfaithfulness and divorce."

"I held Ashfield."

"And on Friday, December 3, 1926 . . ."

"Since August 1926, obedience had not, silence had not, and on December 3, 1926, fighting did not work. Archie walked out and went to her. Despite . . ."

"The fight you put up. You thought you could win with Archie as you had with your mother. You believed if you fought and won it was a sign you were good, or at least right, probably a sign you were loved."

"Yes! The goodness and correctness and rightness *prevail.* Love means caring about the feelings of another."

"Winning proved your goodness and could obliterate shame and fear and loss, obliterate The Gun Man. If The Gun Man is your worthless, unlovable side. But when you lost the fight with Archie . . ."

"What?"

"To win the infrequent times you fought was to dispel fear, shame, and loss. To lose was to be overwhelmed by them."

"Shame, loss, fear. The loss is obvious, my mother and my husband within months of one another. The shame is obvious; losing your husband to another woman is somehow your own fault, a sign of your failure as a wife. But *what* was the fear?"

"Your first articulated fear is The Gun Man. I don't understand it yet, but The Gun Man is evil."

"Hah! Proof I was no good? Only a *facade* of worth and decency with evil up my sleeve like The Gun Man? If I were good, deserving, I would win? So, you are suggesting The Gun Man may be a sort of dream code for my fear that my true and hidden nature is worthless or evil, unlovable. Well, for all your fancy degrees, you have come to the same conclusion as the Surrey and Berkshire constabularies." She grabbed her purse and rummaged through it with a vengeance. "Look!" She was waving a scrap of newspaper. "Here is one cutting you do not have in your scrapbook." She read aloud. "December 19, 1926: Col. Christie Refuses To Pay Hunt Expenses; Police Send Him Bill For Twenty-five Pounds; Outlay By Them In Search For His Wife." She almost threw it at me. "Twenty-five pounds! How more clearly could they have accused me of shamming? How could they make it more plain that they thought I orchestrated the whole thing? A thousand pounds, ten thousand pounds, and I could walk upright, but twenty-five pounds is a slap in the face, or on the wrist. And now you, you think my secret is I am The Gun Man, the evil person; *you* think I planned it all. Oh I can see the clues to *your* inner meaning as easily as you see mine. I was ashamed by Archie's affair. I meant to have my way. He denied me and went to her, and I went off to show him, to worry and embarrass him in print, and force him to come after me. You and the damn bobbies! If there is perfect symmetry in the real world, your bill will probably be twenty-five pounds. Well, close your notebook and pull out your charge book. Archie refused to pay them, but I will pay you and be done with you this instant!"

"I wonder why you want to believe you are the culprit."

"*I, I* want to believe?"

"Well, yes. Neither of us yet know what happened and you keep pressing *your* favorite solution."

"But it was *you . . .*"

"I only said you fought to beat The Gun Man, and The Gun Man is a dream symbol of evil. You fought to dispel evil. You take any fact and insist it means you are the culprit. You press that interpretation when I am still trying to *find* all the facts and then the truth."

"Well, well, you are Poirot and I am Hastings."

"It must be hard to think how readily Archie paid twenty-five pounds to marry you and a decade later would not part with twenty-five pounds to save you from public humiliation. It was not the fee, but his refusal to pay, that made the press. You knew that and knew it meant you were an unloved wife. Memory itself is a kind of admission."

"Yes, it is."

"Owning your true past may be the hardest thing you ever do. Most people never do it. We all have memories of things we have done or have been done to us that we would rather forget. Most people pare down their memories, drop parts off along the way, reshape the memories they keep in order to tell the story of their life the way they want it to have been. They foist their well-tailored memories upon others as if to say, *what a good person I am and have always been.* At least you have the courage to admit

61

there are some memories so damning you *can't* remember them."

She stood with her back to me. I imagine she was once more prepared to leave. For the first time I called her Agatha, leaned forward, and touched the back of her arm. "Agatha, *whatever* it is that you have been afraid to remember for so long, whoever it shows you were in the past, remembering will show you to be a person of great courage here and now."

"You are restraining me."

"I hope not. I hope you are restraining yourself from running away again."

"Again?"

"Again. Isn't amnesia a method of running away? Isn't there a pattern in your life of running from ugliness?"

"Pattern . . . logic. We have the pieces, the clues, don't we already have the solution? I had lost a mother and was threatened with losing a husband. I would fight to stem loss. I would become willful, combative, to gain my way. I would think my very life depended upon it, so I would do anything to stop Archie." She turned and faced me, considering. "Anything. It is logical. Logic tells us that is who I was in 1926 and I created a scandal to, to . . ."

"To what?"

"*Something.* To have my way, then forget the kind of person I was."

We were getting so close. A person willing to accuse herself is often very close to acknowledging the truth. Self-accusation is a last ditch stand. A person hopes for society's formula response, "Oh, no dear, of course you are not to blame," followed by an end to further discussion. But if that is not the response, the person knows the risk is having to go on until the truth is told.

"Human beings are not always logical. You said yourself, the most likely suspect is not always guilty. Therefore, the logical answer is not always the true one. The reader should not accept the logical one and stop thinking." I paused. She was still turned away from me. "This isn't working," I said.

"At last," she turned. "Détente."

"It needs to be a collaboration."

"You have said that before."

"Yes, and I meant it. I just didn't do it," I admitted.

"This has been exactly as much of a collaboration as a good meal if you are the diner and I am the mutton chop."

I laughed. "A description of Freudian psychoanalysis? And you know what's wrong with it?"

"At the end of the meal, you are satisfied and I have disappeared."

That stopped me. "What did you say?"

She sat. "You are satisfied, I have disappeared."

"I was going to say, it takes away your power and initiative." I stopped to write the word 'disappeared' on a note and put it in my pocket. "You need to solve this."

"But I remember *nothing*—nothing, that is the point."

Obviously, she believed therapy was both painful and time consuming. She had solved the latter problem by promising to give me no more than one afternoon. She was so resolute in her expectation of pain that she was grasping at any possible source of pain including self-incrimination. She was not finding true memories; she was fashioning painful explanations. If I was to break through, I had to give her the opportunity to discuss the events of the lost days without evoking either the pain or resistance. My solution was to use her strength. She excelled at story-telling. Let her tell the events as if they were happening to a character in a book. Let her take control of the session.

"I accept that you remember nothing." I tapped my scrapbook. "We have the facts here in the news accounts. We will lay out the facts, and you, the writer of mysteries, will do . . . whatever it is you do."

"Just as if it were one of my sausages."

"Sausages?"

"It is what I call my books, sausages."

"As in bringing home the bacon?"

"That is really very good. I wish I had thought of it, but, no, as in cranking them out link after link."

"Then it is agreed?"

"We set the plot with the facts we know . . ."

"And you solve your mystery as if it were happening to a character, to someone else."

"I have to have apples."

"Apples." Apples? I got up and started rummaging until I found a bag of unknown provenance.

"I eat apples when I write; it helps me think. I lay in a supply preparatory to starting a book."

I turned the bag upside down, and three or more apples dropped into her lap. "Apples," I said.

She bobbled the apples to keep them from falling. "It will have to be a short book."

"But now we have a deal?"

"Agreed."

I was turning the therapeutic process on its head in, I hoped, a good cause. If she freely discussed the events of the eleven lost days, in her style, perhaps she could find the courage to own them. *Claiming* memory, *reclaiming* memory, are, after all, acts of ownership.

4

The Artist

*There is a debate about whether psychology
is art or science. Like many debates it wastes
precious energy because the answer is:
it is both. Like all sciences, psychology
requires a special language and knowledge
base. In practice, it requires that which
art requires: love of the task
and a moment of inspiration.*

Agatha set to work. She was tidying up. Papers were neatly stacked on the desk. Other surfaces were cleared. I watched her arrange the last bits on the desk, carefully leaving an empty space in the center. She pulled my chair around and sat behind my desk. Then she carefully filled the empty space with blank paper, two pencils, and the apples stacked in a neat pyramid.

By way of explanation, she said, "I could not see how you were able to work in this mess."

"You like your world neat, everything in its proper place."

"Yes, that may be what writing is, tidying up the information, and making all the facts fit the solution."

"No loose ends."

I looked around for a place to sit, and selected the chair she had occupied. It was a clear rebalancing of the power in the room. It was the rules of her profession, not mine, that would control. So far, it was a good plan. Her speech was bright. She was more mobile, her gestures wider. She was very much in charge.

"Right. Now. First," she instructed me, "we recite the facts and state the mystery so the reader knows where we are."

"And where we have to go." I felt I should make some contribution.

She selected an apple and took a bite. "Quite."

I took up the scrapbook and began. "Fact one. In 1926, the author, Agatha Christie, disappeared from her home."

"No extraneous bits. Pare down. What difference does it make that she was an author? This might have been a purely personal act."

"If she were Jane Doe working in a sausage factory, others would not have reacted as they did and it would change the facts in the case. Further, as a person, she would have different concerns."

"Well alright, go on then."

"Her car was found abandoned at the side of a road in Surrey, at Newland Corners. The road was little more than a lane, and at a point where it both descended and curved, her car had gone off the track and rested against a tree."

"Won't do. Here we need specifics. Was it day or night? April or January? I mean, if she left the house on a summer afternoon, where's the mystery? One can imagine nothing more sinister than a pleasant outing, a picnic, say."

"It was after dark, the first week in December."

"Now you have said something. Why would anyone venture out at such a time?"

"Further, when she left the car, her fur coat remained. Almost simultaneously, she was reported missing from her home in one police jurisdiction, and her car was found miles away in a different police jurisdiction."

"Pare down. Why do we care about jurisdictions?"

"I don't know. I'm just telling it." I felt as if I were on a seesaw: pare down, add more. Perhaps the secret of good storytelling was having a sense of just how much to tell. She said nothing so I went on. "The abandoned car was found by a father and child out for an early morning walk who reported it to the Surrey police; her disappearance from home was reported at almost the same hour to the Berkshire police. Oh, that's jurisdictions again. Well, strike the last part."

"No, I see, too many cooks. Gives our detective a clear field while the petty jurisdictional competition rages on and the constables trip over one another. Records lost and incomplete; each jurisdiction thinking the other had noted it down or taken charge of it."

"Very clever. Did that happen?"

"What comes next?"

"Mrs. Christie is an extraordinarily popular writer. Her fame and popularity combined with the mysterious disappearance occasioned a national frenzy of police activity and newspaper coverage. At one point, 15,000 volunteers were in the fields near the abandoned car searching for clues."

She waved it away. "We've been all over that bit. Let's have the theories."

"The theories. Well, in the first hours, accident or suicide was feared. When no body and no clues were found, it was postulated that she had been kidnapped. When no note for ransom arrived, it was suggested the foul men who acted for profit had bungled the thing and murdered her inadvertently. Finally, her husband Archie was suspected of deliberate murder to gain his freedom in

71

order to marry one Nancy Neele. After a week, the concerned were joined by the cynics, who wrote that Mrs. Christie was in hiding voluntarily for the purpose of promoting her book sales."

"That last won't do as a motive. I mean, it is back logic. You can't say because *later* book sales went up . . ."

"Did they?"

"Positively soared!" She smiled and returned to business. "Nevertheless, you can not say that since a thing happened *later*, it was intended *earlier*. I mean, how was I to know, *she* to know?"

"Next theory: to punish her errant husband?"

"Same argument. People are always saying if I do this, he will do that. Well, anything might happen. Now with murder, you say, if I kill him, he will be dead. Pretty certain. But if I kick him, he will fly through the air? Pretty uncertain. He may stand firm, absorb the kick, and hit you in the head. Archie, that is the husband, had another woman, he might have said, 'good, the wife is gone.' In fact that is more logical than thinking he would drop his mistress and go bounding after an unwanted wife."

"After eleven days, Agatha Christie was found sitting in the lobby of the Hydropathic Hotel at Harrogate. She had arrived in conventional fashion by train from London. Unconventionally, she had registered under the name of Theresa Neele. Archie was brought by the police to identify her."

She laughed. "Well, yes, he identified me, but I could not identify *him*. I did not know who he was when he walked up to me in the lobby; I guessed he was . . ." She stopped, and then said, "well, in any case, I did not know him."

I wrote "who?" and put the note in my pocket. "Only one statement was given to the press: Mrs. Christie has suffered from amnesia. No questions were entertained. The world balked. Amnesia indeed."

"Well, well, all the nice theories in the press, and in the end the public is cheated. No juicy murder, obviously; I am still here. No dastardly kidnapping. A disappointed public reconsiders: yesterday's possible victim branded the probable culprit. What was the old girl up to? They didn't *like* amnesia as an answer; got to give the public what it wants or it turns on you."

"Are you being too hard on the public? It is 1946, and I have never before seen a genuine case of amnesia. In 1926 . . ."

"Well if I am your first psychiatric patient, how does that signify? How many cases of any kind have you seen?"

"I only meant the public would find the explanation as mysterious as the disappearance."

She took another bite of apple and chewed vigorously. "Yes, yes, and the solution should be clear and easy to swallow." She swallowed.

"So, the old mystery (what happened to Agatha Christie) was not solved. It was replaced. The new mystery was: had it been amnesia, or a conscious act, and in either case, why? What next?" I asked.

"Go back a bit. The car was found off the road. Now that is the thing I am best at."

"Wrecking cars?"

"I see you intend to have a good time and let me work."

"I do," I agreed amiably.

"What I am best at is telling the reader exactly, I may say precisely, what was said or done, and letting the reader mislead himself."

"How?"

"Well, all actions are subject to interpretation."

"Hope so, or I am out of a job."

"The trick is more than one interpretation fits any single action. The motor car was found off the road against a tree. Why?"

I tried my best Hastings. "Well, it was a narrow road, dark, December, maybe a slippery road. I conclude, an accident."

"Sound guess. Now say the woman reappears and says she had amnesia. Amnesia *hides* something, past memories, from the person herself, but what if she wants to hide something from everyone else? We don't know she *had* amnesia, we only know she *said* she did. All she has to do is allow or encourage people to think about the motor against the tree, assume accident, and *voilà!*, amnesia is explained and accepted. Then, *découverte!*, the detective does his stuff, and it is discovered she faked amnesia and pushed the motor car against the tree!"

"Did you?" She ignored my question, and continued theorizing.

"Then you ask, why did she? It was dark and a narrow track. If the motor stalled, she could not leave it in the road, it was too narrow. Or, if she wanted to avoid detection, same reason. Or, if she skidded off the road and then wanted to make sure her motor did not roll any further down the slick embankment, or if she planned to commit a crime and did not want to use her own motor, what better, in every case, than for her to roll it off the road against a tree? That is the secret."

"To the position in which your car was found?"

"No, the secret to fooling my readers. Step one is multiple interpretations, all possible, all logical. Step two is a bit of misdirection, her lie about amnesia. The reader *leaps* to the wrong conclusion until the very end."

"So, to solve your mystery stories, you have to fit the clues together. Relying on any one gets you into trouble."

She nodded, chewed, and got up to deposit the apple core neatly into the wastepaper basket. "Everything in its place," she said. "Fit *all* clues together, no loose ends."

"Ahh," I checked my clippings. "What next?"

"The mink coat left in the car."

"That action fits with . . ."

"Either," she said definitively. "Consistent with an accident, disorientation, she wanders off without her belongings. *And,* consistent with wanting consciously to disappear; purposefully leaving behind conspicuous personal belongings like a car or an expensive coat that someone in her home will notice is gone and know she is wearing."

I skimmed. "What next?"

"The train to Harrogate," she said. "Now that *is* strange."

"Why?"

"One can not seem to write a mystery or solve one in England without an A.B.C. railway guide; but if my memory serves . . ."

At that she threw down her pencil and laughed. "Well, you know what I mean. The train she took to London was from the Guilford Station."

"You arrived in Harrogate off the London line."

"So she had to get to London. Then *why* was her car found at Newland Corners? That is the real significance of the two jurisdictions; it is a clue to how far she drove."

"It is?"

"Yes. You see, from her home, Styles in Sunningdale, Guilford Station is *before* Newland Corners. The Morris was found miles *past* Guilford Station. Moreover, there was a London line in Berkshire, a mile from her home." She interrupted herself to select another apple. "You know, I believe that is another way I fool my readers. I tell them the only important thing about the two jurisdictions is that my detective has a clear field and will get there first. Well, it sounds logical, the reader accepts it, and *stops* thinking about it, you see? Doesn't ask himself, what else could it mean? Or ask himself, just because it is logical, does that make it true?"

"So now we have the *true* significance of the jurisdictions? You drove from your house in Sunningdale, miles *past* the Berkshire line to London and *past* Guilford Station, stopped for whatever reason, left the car, and *walked* back to Guilford?"

"Must have done."

"Well, in terms of the overall mystery, amnesia or calculated action, it would seem . . ."

"Consistent with either. Consciously wants to 'cover her tracks' and 'doubles back,' as you Yanks would say, conscious fear of being followed or found, *or* she does not remember where either station is because she has amnesia."

"Poirot?"

She was scribbling and chewing, and only gave me a "Mmmm?"

Even with the protection of storytelling, she was ignoring my factual questions, spinning theory. "We do *not* progress."

She was so engrossed in her-life-as-fiction that she had now progressed to ignoring me entirely. I was only given another, "Mmmm."

I tried again. "Don't you see, you could spin interpretations all day? It is what you do, probably better than anyone alive."

"Possibilities. Archie said just that: I could think of more possibilities than anyone alive. Archie could only ever think of one, and he was always certain it was the right one. Only one thing to be done, and then he would do it."

I capitulated. At least she was involved and talking. "Alright, what next?"

"The police bring Archie to Harrogate. Whatever I may be guilty of, I really did not recognize Archie in the lobby of the Hydro when the police brought him to identify me. That argues for amnesia. But, then I, she, registered as Theresa Neele. Nancy Neele was the name of Archie's lover. I did not know my name, but I knew the surname of my husband's lover? Argues against amnesia."

"We know you knew a Neele. Did you know a Theresa?"

"When I was young, I knew a Teresa at Torquay."

"Where Ashfield is; perhaps her last name was Neele. Amnesia can play tricks and old memories can remain, although disjointed, when obvious things like your own name are erased."

"Yes, I remember a Teresa who lived at Torquay, in Devonshire, near Ashfield, but I can't remember her last name."

"Teresa of Torquay was from childhood, before Archie. You might have been symbolically escaping Archie."

"No, no, that is your brand of voodoo. May serve as a red herring. Constables running here and there searching for a Teresa late of Devonshire who turns out to be . . . never mind, my readers would never accept it. Has to be straightforward when revealed."

"Wasn't there a *Saint* Teresa? A mystic?"

"Yes, the Carmelite. Wait. Ste. Thérèse, the Little Flower. She was canonized in 1925. I *might* have been thinking of her in 1926. But neither saint's name is spelt the same way I spelt Theresa Neele."

"You use children's games and rhymes in your books and in the titles. Simple and childlike clues."

"Yes. Word games. Always have done. Like *The Blue Beard of Unhappiness* or *Why Did They Bag-Dad?*"

"Bird? Baghdad?"

"No, not b-i-r-d, b-e-a-r-d. I admit I pronounced it to rhyme with 'herd.' Cheating a little, but in parts of England they do pronouce it like that. It means facial hair, but also the barb of an arrow. See? If stuck with a barb, one would be unhappy." She took a bite of apple, thoroughly enjoying herself. "And it's not *Bagh*dad, but bag *Dad*. You see, go hunting to bag an animal, crudely put, *kill*, or go hunting and bag *Dad*. Titles of my early work, *very* early, mercifully unpublished, works. Word play. Playing with meaning. You should be pleased we are back into my childhood once again." She took the last bite of apple and tossed it into the basket. Direct hit; as if memories of childhood prompted a childlike act. "Wait a bit. What did you say about saints? T-h-e-r-e-s-e and T-e-r-e-s-a. The registration card at The Hydro said T-H-e-r-e-s-a Neele of Good Hope, South Africa. Maybe I had a reason for the spelling. Maybe it was like an acrostic or *The Times* demon crossword? I have to think. The simplest part is: *Good hope (one word, four letters)*. Guess, it's easy."

"You mean a good hope? A word with four letters? Wait. Wish?"

"Yes." It delighted her that I got it in one. "Now, Theresa, that's harder. T..H..E..R..E..S..A. Let's see, much harder. No, I have it, it is like the demon crossword. *Good hope, Theresa. Must have Latin.*" 1 word, 7 letters."

"Good hope is wish."

She was impatient with me. "We have that part." No points for past glories.

"Teresa, the childhood friend, or Saint Teresa, a writer like you, or Ste. Thérèse the Little Flower?"

"No, be literal. The answer is a Latin word. The clue says: *from the Latin; must have Latin*. Do you see it now?"

"'Fraid not."

She almost clapped her hands with glee. " *The* rasa, as in tabula rasa, you know, blank slate. Phrase, three words, wish the blankness. Answer: Latin word, 7 letters; *Amnesia!*"

"You registered at the Hydropathic Hotel in a word code that informed whoever did *The Times* demon crossword that you had amnesia?"

"Well, *all* my ideas aren't good. Anyway, whatever way one spells Theresa is wrong. Tabula rasa is r..a..s..a. It doesn't work."

"I am relieved. I never could do *The London Times* crossword."

Such ineptitude was not dignified with a response. She went on. "What is the simplest? Theresa, Theresa. That's it! Just how it sounds. To erase a . . . erase a memory; amnesia. Erase a Neele. It works! Wish to erase a Neele! Oh, no. I must have been mad!" A moment ago, she had happily taken up another apple. Now she raised her hand as if she could ward off the thought, the apple rolled out of her spread fingers onto the floor.

"Stop! Relax, this is conjecture."

The apple remained on the floor between us. Agatha was not listening. "Erase a memory, amnesia; erase a person, murder; erase oneself, suicide. Erase." She looked at me. "It is not *if* I had amnesia, it is *when*. Suppose I went to Harrogate in full possession of my senses to erase *someone;* Nancy or myself? I could imagine murder. I imagine murders daily for a living. Or suicide? I had lost everything, even my pride. In the circumstance, it is possible. I was found, discovered, before I could do it. Ashamed, I wanted to forget my evil intent, and I did. It was only *then,* when found, that I got amnesia."

"Good plot. I believe you published it under the

pseudonym Mary Westmacott." It was time to move away from fiction.

"My word, you are a wonder! No one, absolutely no one knows I publish under that name."

"Oh, how hard it is to resist saying, *elementary*."

"Do not let the competition stand in your way."

"Elementary, my dear . . . lady. In *Unfinished Portrait* by Mary Westmacott, the young wife runs from her home to water, a bridge not a spa. She attempts to jump off because her husband has betrayed her. A man discovers her before she succeeds, and without either knowing the other's name, she tells him the story of her life and the betrayal that led her to the bridge, to the brink of suicide. After talking it all out, she determines to live. Whether she actually forgets the episode, she determines never to speak of it again."

"You think that is what happened? I went to Harrogate to die?"

"Nope. You invent plots and possibilities. *Unfinished Portrait* was just one more. In my opinion, it is true in one respect: talking might have made you well. I think *Unfinished Portrait* was true in another respect. You could not talk. The strictures against talking about private matters were too strong. In the book, you make a kind of joke of a serious problem. Your heroine goes to her first formal party, and a man says to her mother, *Your daughter has learnt to dance, in fact she dances beautifully. You had better try and teach her to talk now.* And in the book your heroine is only able to talk if the other person does not know her name, does not know who she is. You were never taught to talk, Agatha."

"That is how you knew I was Mary Westmacott?"

"No. You used a passage from the Bible in a Westmacott book and in a book published under your own name."

"Psalm 55."

"Yes. You changed the wording of the psalm in the same way both as Agatha Christie and as Mary Westmacott. It was too strong a coincidence."

From memory Agatha quoted, "If you had told me that you were my enemy, I would have known to hide from you; if you had told me you meant to attack me, I would have known to defend myself; but you were my ally *my husband, my best friend.*"

"I think that is what you were feeling in December 1926, about Archie. His affair was an attack, the act of an enemy. You were more hurt, angry, and frightened then ever in your life, and you had no outlet because you could not talk about shameful things like divorce, or unpleasant things like fear and loss."

"My mother recanted and kept Ashfield when I fought for it. Archie and I fought, but Archie did not recant. What was I prepared to do? *What*, if I thought my world, my life was at stake and I had no outlet?"

"The fact that you still phrase it in question form means we do not know yet."

"So there is hope. Of what?! That *maybe* I am not a person I would detest if I faced myself?"

"Whatever you are running from is indeed horrid in your own mind, your own opinion."

"Not whatever. Whomever. Myself."

"I agree this is a mystery about identity, just as your

early shame was about identity. Yet it was not directly *your* identity."

"Now what?"

I took scrap after scrap of paper out of my breast-pocket and sorted through. "I have a list here." I was trying to get the notes I had taken in order. "When you first came, you accused me of curing a common cold by demanding that the patient stop sniveling, remember?"

She nodded and asked, "As bad as all that? We are right back to diagnosis: cold; treatment plan: stop sniveling?"

"Eh?" I finished ordering my notes. "Oh, no. I know now."

"You know what happened?" I couldn't tell if she sounded excited or frightened at the prospect.

"That would be putting it too strongly. But I know what questions to ask, and I know we will find the truth when I have the answers."

"Just like in my books. How satisfying. But whom are you going to ask? It is not as if there were any third party to confirm . . ."

"Don't say anything."

"End collaboration?"

"Look. I have learned a lot from you, and I think I can use it to help you. But it is important you not go on pretending the events of the eleven days are fiction." I mentally crossed my fingers for luck. "You have always lied about parts. I don't want you to lie anymore, or fictionalize, not here, not now, not to me. It is of the utmost importance that you do not lie."

She drew herself up like the Victorian grande dame

she was. "I am not aware I have any particular secret that compels me to lie, and I certainly am *not* a liar."

"It won't work, Agatha. That all-concealing, all-powerful social mask you learned at your mother's knee; so opaque anything can hide behind it. It has no power. No. It has great power, but I have discovered yours is a glass mask."

She repeated, "Glass mask," in a way that made me think *she* was going to make a note and put it in her pocket.

"Throughout your life, there were things you dared not say, or chose not to say. At those times your only course was silence. Except, I suspect, there were instances when your prescient mother and granny guessed what was troubling you and said it for you. In 1926, however, both were gone. There was something you could not say, dared not even *think*. The only course was forgetfulness."

"In a civilized world, one does not go about saying just everything. Furthermore, omission is hardly the same thing as lying."

"If the listener, or your reader, accepted the partial story for the whole, that was not your fault?"

Agatha nodded.

"I should not have used the word *lied*. Yankee directness is rudeness here in England. May I apologize? I meant omitted."

"No doubt about the omissions. I seem to have left out eleven days at a pop."

"I was thinking of something more specific. You left three notes before you disappeared on that December night. Significant clues; yet you never mentioned them in your reconstruction just now."

"Oh, well, notes. *Alleged* notes." She waved away notes. "One to Archie's brother which he could not find. One to Archie which *he* could not find. The only one we know existed is the one to my secretary, Miss Fisher. She produced it. Everyone who read it said that, with the exception of one purely domestic instruction, it was gibberish, hardly worth mentioning."

"I see. Then will you hear my list of questions?"

"Exactly like Poirot."

"The first: are your three notes worth mentioning?" I smiled, then spoke with growing seriousness. "What did you *not* tell your mother about The Gun Man dream? Why do you speak of the events of 1926 as if you are going *toward* them when they are twenty years in your past? Why did you say it was "cheek" for your brother Monty to smile at the birthday table in your dream? Why were you angry at Madge for saying, *Poor Mummy*?

"Why did The Gun Man dream stop when you were twelve? Why do you make a point of telling me where you were sitting when Archie told you about Nancy Neele? Do you include seemingly unimportant detail to obscure what you did not tell me about that day at Ashfield, or was the spot important? Who did you think Archie was in the lobby of the Hydropathic Hotel? Why do we seem always to end by talking about disappearance? The Gun Man appears at the birthday table, and disappears when you wake. You fear you will disappear in the therapeutic process. You disappeared from Styles for eleven days. Well, that will do for a start."

85

"You must have your chair back." She got up and moved from behind the desk. "Clearly, you are going to write the ending to the story."

"No, Agatha, you are going to tell me the answers. What happened in the lost days? What shamed you and frightened you so much that you ran away, lost yourself and lost your memory?"

"We are back where we started. Circles. You go in circles."

"Now we are armed. Now you can tell me."

"We?"

"You are right. I am armed. I know now how to protect you, and from what."

"What? What could be so terrible that I erased my memory for twenty years?"

Luckily that was one question on the list to which I had the answer, not just a reasonable guess. "Disappearing. Losing yourself; or some significant part of yourself. I will not let that happen, I can protect you. Trust me."

"Let us suppose I trust you, the Yankee Clipper on his maiden voyage, *how* do I remember? *How* can you be sure I will remember everything and tell you the truth, the whole truth?"

"Will you trust me?" I got up and started to move around the room.

Her eyes followed me. "Well, I suppose I must."

I turned off the lights one by one. I sat with a pin light in my hand. "Will you?"

"Oh, very well. I suppose, actually, I do."

I moved it in an arc before her eyes. "You are completely relaxed. You will see the events of your life as if in a motion picture. You will see the events but be untouched by them. You will be interested but unaffected. Concentrate on the light. You are getting sleepy. Very, very sleepy. Soon you will sleep, and when you do you will remember; find your voice; tell your story; leave nothing out. Now Agatha, you are asleep."

5

The Mesmerist

*G. Mesmer (1737–1815) was a
French physician who perfected hypnotism
as a treatment tool. His name
became synonymous with the technique.
Hypnotizing and mesmerizing
are synonymous.*

"When you sleep, you will remember. Agatha, can you hear me?"

"Yes."

"How do you feel?"

"Just fine."

"You are very young. You are five years old. You are in your bed. You are having a happy dream about your birthday party. Tell me the story about the dream."

She smiled. "Yes. We are at the table at Ashfield; everyone is waiting for me to make a wish, and blow out my candles."

"Next something frightening happens in your dream."

She tensed.

"It is alright. In a second, The Gun Man will appear at the table."

She was still rigid.

"This time will be different. You will not be shocked because you are prepared, you know what is coming. You will not be afraid because you are just telling me the story."

She relaxed.

"Here he comes. He is taking his seat at the birthday table. I can see him and I am not afraid of The Gun Man. Tell me the story of what happens next."

"You are not afraid of The Gun Man?" she asked.

"Not in the least. Neither are you. You are the story-teller. What happens next after he walks up to the table?"

"That's not right!"

"No? I am trying very hard to get it right. Help me. You tell what you see."

"The Gun Man is already at the table."

"Is he now." She had surprised me. "Explain it to me, Agatha."

"Monty is smiling like everyone else, waiting for me to blow out my candles. I look at each person in turn and when I look at him, I see him change into The Gun Man. Monty *becomes* The Gun Man. His mask falls away and I can see the steely eyes. I know the gun is up his sleeve. It is terrible!" She pressed her hands over her eyes.

"You are safe; it is all long ago. You can take away your hands and look."

She let her hands fall and spoke more slowly. "The face he shows everyone else, the smiling brother-face is only his mask. All at once I know he is The Gun Man."

"Only you can see Monty change? Only you know he is really The Gun Man?"

"Yes. Only I see his brother-mask fall. Only I see The Gun Man beneath."

"You are awake from the dream now. Soon your mother will come and sit on your bed. Will you tell your mother that Monty is The Gun Man?"

"No, she would not believe me. Anyway she would not like to hear me say such a thing."

"I understand. The Gun Man is scary, but you do not feel afraid just now. Now, you are only telling the story of things that happened long ago. They may have scared you then, but the *memory can not harm you.* I will count to three, and when I do, you will wake. You will remember what you have told me, and you will feel refreshed. One, two, three."

"Monty was at all your childhood birthday parties?"

"Yes."

"Did something happen at a real party that caused you to think of him as The Gun Man?"

"There *was* an interminable argument at one party sustained by my brother about how many eclairs he should be allowed to eat. Went on and on; spoiled the whole party, greedy boy."

"Very vexing of him, but not *so* terrible, not Gun Man material, was it?"

"Well, perhaps not."

"Monty did something far worse than that. Something no one but you knew about. Am I right?"

"Do you find you have many friends?"

"Friends?"

"I was just wondering how many people there were who wanted to go about with you and be seen right through at every turning. You see too much."

"You said that once before."

"No less true now."

"So there *was* something Monty did to you that you told no one."

"Fine, unto Caesar. But prepare to be disappointed. It was just silly, and besides, it was all my fault."

I waited.

"Monty invited me on an outing, boating on Torbay

in his dinghy. Unusual that. Most of the time he was telling me to go away. We are sailing over the waves. Ridiculous how delighted I am just because I have been invited to come along by my older brother. Then I get sick; absolutely green. I am hanging over the side of the boat, and Monty is disgusted with me. End of outing. When I am delivered back to Mother, I hear Monty tell her, *Agatha fed the fishes and could not stop.*"

"Don't stop short. Tell the whole story."

"Oh for heaven's sake, I suppose you will go on until you have every little bit, but I warn you, you will be disappointed. Monty had said something like that to me when we were alone in the boat, but when he said it to Mother, he changed the words slightly. To me, he had said, *If you do not stop being sick, I will feed you to the fishes.*"

"You took his words literally?"

"I was terrorized on the way in. I prayed not to be sick again, and mercifully, I was too scared to be sick."

"So you thought he meant it literally. He would throw you overboard if you could not stop vomiting."

"I was a child. Once a farmer caught us picking his fruit and shouted, *if I catch you I will boil you in oil.* I ran like the wind, and was weeks wondering in horror what it would *feel* like to be boiled in oil. I told you it was silly what Monty *did* to me. I was silly to be afraid."

"You are always ready to take the blame. I suppose you couldn't swim?"

"Not any distance. If thrown overboard, I would have quietly slid under the water and disappeared."

"Disappeared?"

"Died. When I was a child I thought of death as disappearing. Not bad, really, for a child. I had determined that dying was when you were not there anymore. When you were dead, no matter how hard people looked for you, you were not there anywhere anymore. Childish, but true enough." She started. "Oh! That is one of the questions on your list. Does that mean when I disappeared in 1926, I *was* planning suicide?"

"Slowly, we are sneaking up on 1926 slowly. Don't run ahead. Unless you are *remembering* what you felt in 1926."

"No, it just seemed to make sense."

"Leave it, then. You said yourself that a logical explanation is not always a true one. I was wondering something more immediate. Did you have any reason for thinking Monty would harm you?"

"Harm me!" The idea seemed to amaze her. She thought a moment. "Oh, I see, if I couldn't swim, pushing me overboard would indeed harm me. Well, at *five years old*, I thought . . . a few days before, Monty had called me a scrawny chicken. It made me cry. I ran to Mother. Mother said, *If you do not want to be teased, why do you go trailing after Monty all the time?* To this day, I don't know the answer. Monty was irresistible to me even though I was a nuisance to him. I followed him everywhere. I suppose my five-year-old reasoning was that he would throw me overboard to be rid of me. So you see, it was my fault because I could not stay away and leave Monty in peace when he wanted it. And I hope you see this is very silly. The child may be father to the man, and all that mumbo-jumbo to which you and your brethern subscribe, but the problem is, childish ideas really are childish."

95

"There is one part that is not childish or silly at all. It is, in fact, sophisticated. The Gun Man was a person who was not who he seemed, wore a mask, that you saw slip away."

"Yes, I dreamt I was sitting with my family, perfectly at ease, and all at once, the mask slips. I see a trusted and loved family member become The Gun Man. I see him for what he really is."

"What does The Gun Man remind you of?"

"*Beware the false prophets who come to you in sheep's clothing but inwardly are ravening wolves.* Something of the sort."

"Like the hypocrites in the Bible who appear outwardly beautiful but inwardly are full of inequity?"

"Yes. The Gun Man is exactly that."

"You said Monty changed his words only slightly from what he said to you and to your mother. He knew what he was doing. He was making himself appear the good brother. One who had taken care of a sick little sister, taken her safely ashore out of concern. You knew he was not being truthful. When you were sick, he was not sympathetic; he was disgusted with you and your sickness. He threatened and frightened you. In daylight you could not tell your mother what he really had said. At night you dreamt of the hypocrite who was your brother. Not so childish. In fact, it was very sophisicated to observe the difference in the two sentences and understand its significance. You used it as an adult writer. It is a concept that has kept you in kippers."

"The character who has done the dastardly yet successfully ingratiates himself even with the mourners—the least likely suspect. I used it for years in my books yet The Gun Man dreams stop when I am twelve. Why?"

"You were not angry at your father for how he left you and your mother financially, were you?"

"No. You were wrong about that."

"Yes, I was, wasn't I? According to the books, everything is supposed to be the fault of the parents: laid at their feet or at least traced to their door. I may have overtrained." I pulled at my ear thinking about the difficulties of discriminating between psychological theories rather than accepting the lot.

"Not true in my case?"

"Not altogether," I said. "The death of your father was very sad, and being reduced to poverty was scary, but your father was no Gun Man."

"Certainly not. I said as much."

"You did, but now I understand. The Gun Man is not simply an evil-doer. He is a hypocrite. Your father was not hiding behind a false mask. He never pretended to be what he was not, nor ever intended to do harm."

"No, never. Business bewildered Father, and when things went wrong, he would write dear old so-and-so or dear old somebody to ask what it all meant. A letter would come back reassuring him, saying something deep about market conditions. He never understood a word of it and could not understand what to do to shore up our finances. Father tried, and when it all went wrong, it depressed him very much. We all have failings. He never denied or tried to hide his. He did try to overcome them."

"The Gun Man dreams stopped when you were twelve because you learned bad things could happen in innocent ways. Death is a desertion, but it is not cruelty, not willful desertion. Good men die, and a good man can be a bad businessman."

"So true. That is why I felt angry at Madge for saying *Poor Mummy* over and over. Mother was the manager. Mother was the one who always knew what to do. If there was a problem, Mother was there to solve it, not fall victim to it. Madge was frightening me by making it sound as if Mother was defeated. If that was true, we were utterly lost. Mother did better in reduced circumstances than Father was able to do with a fortune, and no one was surprised."

"Your father and mother were genuinely who they appeared to be. All sad things are not evil things. The evil is in the hypocrisy. The evil is in caring for no one but yourself. When you learned that, The Gun Man dreams stopped."

"Well that is nicely cleared up, and another one ticked off your list."

"The truth pleases you. I was wrong about your father, and having it cleared up is pleasing."

"It is."

"Good. I am counting on that."

"Then you needn't worry. It is like the gas leak."

"Gas . . . ?"

"Leak. When Max and I moved into our house, I smelt gas in our bedroom. No one else smelt it, but it annoyed me. I had the gas man and the builder and I don't know how many in. No one smelt it. They thought I was mad. Oh, they were all patience and condescension as they asked: *have you failed to notice there was no gas in the house; perhaps it is a dead mouse, one is often mistaken for the other?*

We checked and double-checked. I even had the floor-boards up, no mouse . . . nothing. Still I smelt it. I would not give up. I had to find out what I smelt. With everyone begging that I forget all about it, I went on. Finally, I had a man in and he pulled the room apart, and there it was! An old gas pipe, open and leaking! We could have been killed in our beds by fumes. We got it out, and I made myself absolutely unbearable for days, bragging about my *nose*. What fun."

"I will depend upon your deep desire to find the truth."

"Yes, alright, but why?"

"Ambivalence is wanting two mutually exclusive things equally and at the same time."

"Sounds uncomfortable."

"Is it?"

"What do you mean, is it?"

"You have lived wanting to know the truth and not wanting to remember for twenty years."

"Oh!"

"I hope wanting to know wins out. Shall we see? Monty became The Gun Man at the outdoor table at Ashfield."

"Yes, at the table. In a dream, of course, but the table was real enough."

"At the same table at which you and Archie sat when he told you about Nancy Neele."

"I told you that."

"Yes, you did, but why did you?"

"Because it was true."

"No other reason? I notice your narratives are not filled with physical detail. Why mention the exact table?"

She seemed uncomfortable, but only said, "What other reason?"

"I think that was my question."

"Oh very well. Here is where all your theories fall to the ground. The truth is obvious. I am, or was, at that time, your garden variety lunatic. It is why I never told anyone this part before. *Omitted* it. They would just have written me off, there and then, and not gone on to discover the truth. Why would you want to talk to a lunatic?"

"I took a degree in talking to lunatics."

"You know very well what I mean."

"I know that what you said is somewhat contradictory. If the truth is that you went mad, and *they* discover it, why would they stop trying to discover the cause, the cure, the whole truth?"

"It is my belief that *they* consider madness a truth in itself and stop there. Wash their hands."

"Well, I won't stop until you are satisfied, alright?"

She sat nodding and considering. "Here is the rest of the story then. Archie told me we were not going abroad. I was shocked, *Not?* And he said . . ." She stopped.

I fumbled with my notebook and located the right section. I did not want to lose the moment. I gave Archie's answer. "No I tell you. I don't feel like it."

"You mean you want to stay here, at Ashfield?" Again she stopped.

I held my notebook open to the right page and read. "You don't understand."

"Yes. And then he says, *This thing has happened. You*

know that dark girl who used to be Belcher's secretary? We had her down for a weekend once, about a year ago, with Belcher, and we've seen her in London once or twice? Yes, I remember Nancy Neele. And he . . ." Again she stopped.

I rifled madly through, but could not find those sentences. I waited. This was the part she had omitted. At last she supplied the rest.

"*Yes. Well, I have been seeing her since I have been alone in London.*" She looked at me. "*I say, "that's nice.* I actually said, that's nice. Then he says, *Oh, you still do not understand. I have fallen in love with her and I'd like you to give me a divorce as soon as it can be arranged.* All I can think is as far as I knew, Archie never even *liked* her. I sit staring at him unable to take it in. There were no money troubles, no press of business, just shabby lies to get me out of the way so he could conduct an affair with Nancy Neele." She threw her hands over her face. "It is horrid!"

"Is? What *is* horrid, Agatha?" She sat frozen with her hands over her face shaking her head.

"You can tell me the whole story because it was all long ago. It hurt and frightened you then, but the *memory* can not hurt you. Omit nothing." I was about to say tell me what was said, but I thought about her hands over her face, and said, "Tell me what you see."

"Archie, I see Archie, *become* The Gun Man." She almost shrieked it, and added softly, "I must have been mad!"

I was caught up in the answers to my list of questions. "So that is why you told me it was the same table. A clue that it was the same event. Monty became The Gun

101

Man at the table. Archie became The Gun Man at the same table." It was certainly a mistake in focus.

She was justifiably aggrieved. "That is hardly the important part! Forget your list for a moment, can't you? I saw Archie change into The Gun Man and I was *awake, awake!*"

"So you concluded you were mad."

"Stark raving!"

"But he *was* The Gun Man, a stranger beneath the mask of a husband. A traitor, someone you trusted who betrayed you, wounded you, and lied about it."

"Yes, *alright!*" She was angry. "But you do not seem to understand that I must have been hallucinating."

"Hallucinating or seeing clearly? You were facing great loss of the most significant man in your life, not to death, but to desertion. Far worse than death because Archie could *help* it, but *chose* to leave you. At Ashfield, as you sorted through the memorabilia of your entire life, the death of your father became vivid again; the death of your mother was a fresh wound. Realization came: you were an orphan. You momentarily forgot your name because a part of your own identity was dead. Another part of your identity, wife? Archie wanted to undo that. He wanted to divorce and abandon you for another woman when you needed your husband most. He chose to tell you about the affair when you were sad and exhausted. He did all this without, apparently, a pang of conscience, or thought for your feelings."

"You are saying if there is an understandable reason for one's behavior . . ."

"It would have been understandable if you had

picked up the outdoor table at Ashfield and crowned him with it. You sat quietly, seeing him clearly for what he was. You could not say it, but you allowed yourself to *see* it. Unfortunately in choosing that way, you recognized and discounted the knowledge at the same time."

"Wait a bit. You *are* saying, if there is an understandable reason for what happened, it was not mad?"

"That is how we generally define normal behavior."

"Even though I thought I *saw* Archie become The Gun Man."

"It was hard for you to accept Archie for what he was showing himself to be. It was impossible for you to say it. Yet you did see it. You did it in a way that allowed you to see it and immediately deny it. The vision does not make you mad; but it did allow you to be ambivalent."

"*See* Archie for what he was, and then deny it?"

"So you could go on, as your mother always taught you to do."

"It allowed me to go on hoping and trying to save the marriage."

"Which you did."

"So, I may not have been losing my mind; but why did I not lose my memory there and then? After all, I was exhausted and threatened, in shock, and had lost my parents and my husband like the boy you told me about in the case study. He lost his memory immediately."

"Because whatever the thing you could not face, the thing you *had* to forget in order to continue functioning, had not happened yet. Therefore, you did not lose your memory that summer. In December that thing happened and you could not go on."

"After I was found, everyone thought I was shamming; *hysterical,* Harley Street pronounced. *Nothing more to discover,* Harley Street concluded. Then to appease me they gave me a prescription, *Rest and quiet.* Seemed quite sensible to them; sounded rubbish to me."

"That was all?"

"Yes. Well, a bit more. One eminence pronounced it possible that I had suffered spontaneous loss of identity in my home on December 3, and therefore, wandered off into oblivion."

I considered. "A fugue state. A disturbed state, a form of amnesia, presumably caused by an excess of emotional stress. In fugue, a person forgets who he is, wanders off, sets up a new life with a new name, and then functions, apparently normally."

"Making a nonsense of what really happened."

"Their explanation sounded rubbish?" I pulled at my ear. "But you said nothing."

"Nothing at all."

"Saved you from explanations."

"Dreaded explanations."

"Fugue state seems a sound explanation. What troubles you about it?"

Silence.

"If it seemed rubbish to you, I believe it was," I added.

"Do you?"

"Yes." No response. "I promised to believe you."

"Yes, of course, and did except when you were accusing me of lying. One tends not to accuse people of lying."

"Well, yes. I did apologize even though . . ." I started

again. "Accepting your memory loss was genuine, I asked myself, could it be a fugue state or psychogenic amnesia? After all, you were under great stress, death and desertion and fatigue if not outright illness of some variety . . ."

"A heaping on of problems."

"Yes, but then your question is the best one: why didn't you wander off in fugue there and then at Ashfield?"

"Can you tell from how memory came back? It was all of a heap, like a package dropped in my lap. I remembered, seemed to remember, the time at the Hydro, but never could I remember why I left home or what happened on the road to Guilford."

"No, not from how it came back, but by the cause of the loss." I pulled my ear. "I suppose, in England, one doesn't say, *the jig is up.*"

"Hardly, nor if one did, would anyone know what was meant."

"I believe you do." I waited; no response. "I believe you lost your memory *after* you left your home. You knew who you were and where you were going when you left Styles. You did not *wander* away in a fugue state."

"Why so certain?" She was deadly calm, the stillness was in her posture and her voice. I hoped it was because at long last she wanted to be discovered.

"Early on, you told me the question was not *if* you lost your memory, but when. I have been thinking about that since you said it, and at least two things made it seem obvious to me that you left Styles in possession of your memory."

"Which things?" She reached for the last apple.

"Oh, no. This is not fiction. We are not here to

105

dream up six impossible things before breakfast. I tell you, and you will invent six conflicting interpretations. This is you life, and you and I are after what *did* happen, not what could have happened. Are you ready to remember? Shall we go behind the wall?"

"And find the leaky gas pipe?"

"Yes."

"Or no leaky gas pipe," she said. "Help me."

I moved around the room turning off the lights. "I will." I took out my pin light. "You are getting sleepy. Soon you will sleep. When you do, it will be December 3, 1926. You will remember everything, but it will be far away, as if you are watching it. You can not be hurt by it, Agatha. Agatha, can you hear me?"

"Yes."

"You are at Styles. It is December 3, 1926. You are fighting with Archie."

"No matter how hard I have tried, he still wants to leave me. I must fight to save my marriage, my home."

She took a breath like a sigh, and continued.

"I tell him, *I can not discuss this now. I can't think. I am ill. Surely you can see that I am ill. Have been since Ashfield.* Archie says, *I did tell you once long ago that I hate it when people are ill or unhappy. It spoils everything for me.*

"*What are you saying?* I ask. He only says, *I must be with Nancy. I can't stand not having what I want, and I can't stand not being happy.*

"I feel as if I am being pulled into a maelstrom, all boundaries, all definition disappearing. *We married in sickness and in health; until death do us part. I do not want a divorce.* I can not reach him. *I will not give you a divorce. I* grope for any common ground. *It would make our daughter very unhappy, and oh Archie, it would make me so very unhappy.* I wait. Then he says, *Everyone can't be happy. Someone has got to be unhappy. Obviously, in this case, it is you.* He seems beyond me as if he has already gone.

"In desperation, I cry out, *But why should it be me who is unhappy and not you?*

"He stands very still and speaks in measured tones as if to an idiot, *As I said: I must be with Nancy. One way or another, I shall be.*" It is a point beyond reason. *My God,* I say. *This will kill me.*"

Agatha began to hyperventilate.

"Agatha, you are perfectly safe. This is only a memory from long ago. Whatever happened then, you have survived it. You can tell me the story without being affected by the events."

She seemed to breathe normally again.

"Archie is gone," I said.

"Yes to her."

"You are at your writing desk."

"Yes, I have a plan." She seemed slightly agitated.

"Good," I told her. "I think it good you have a plan."

"Yes?" She seemed to calm. "Well, yes, perhaps I do too."

"You wrote three letters," I prompted her. "The first was to Miss Fisher."

"She must cancel my reservation at a spa in Yorkshire."

"Then you write Archie's brother."

"Yes. I tell Campbell I am going to a spa in Yorkshire."

"And to Archie?"

"*Archie, You wish that I would disappear and so I have. Agatha.*"

"It is dark outside and cold. You are driving your Morris Cowley. Why are you in the car, Agatha?"

"I have to get away."

"Why?"

"I must."

"The car approaches Newland Corner. The roadway is unlit and narrow. In the morning the car is found off the road against a tree. Did you become upset and lose control of the car?"

"No. I rolled my motor against the tree I . . . I . . . did that . . ." She faltered in the telling.

"You roll the car off the pavement against the tree *on purpose*. Part of your plan." She was becoming agitated again. "It frightens you that you did something, anything *purposefully*."

"Yes."

"It is perfectly normal to do a great many things planfully and purposefully. Why do you roll the car against the tree?"

"I always have trouble parking the Morris on an incline, or a decline for that matter. It would roll; I can not leave the Morris in the roadway . . . too narrow. I have to pull off the roadway. I stop it against a tree to assure it will stay put."

I smiled to myself. "As simple as that. You do give the reader all the clues; fair play." Then to Agatha I said, "Your head is not injured in a car accident?"

"No. Later . . ."

"Your head is injured?"

"No. My knee and leg, my stockings and skirt bloody."

"How?"

"I must be rid of the motor. I turn slowly off the roadway and am trying to drive it gently up against the tree, but it is stuck. In the end, I have to get out and push it the last bit. Ouff!"

"What is it?"

"I trip, bang my knee. I imagine my stocking is torn, but I can not see. Too dark. My knee hurts; it will be harder now to walk to Guilford."

"Why not drive to Guilford? Why abandon the car?"

"I must not be traced; discovered. Archie, the constabulary, so many could identify my motor."

"You must not be found."

She turned and looked over her shoulder. "Not be found." She turns back and peers in front of her.

"What are you doing now?"

"Looking at my coat and handbag on the back seat. I *do* want them, but I realize I can not take them with me."

"Your purse is a means of identification. It identifies you as Agatha Christie."

"Naturally, that is who I am." She considers. "I must leave my handbag."

"I can see that, but why not wear the coat? It is December after all."

"I am so proud of that coat, full-length mink. Oh well, it has to be. A coat like that is conspicuous. Archie could send a description: woman, mid-thirties, last seen wearing a full-length mink."

"You are going to the train?"

"Yes."

"Why not to Sunningdale Station?"

"One could determine my destination from the train I took, and Archie could simply ask the stationmaster. He would recognize me. I am going to Guilford to board the train. My leg is hurting more. I am cold. Worse luck: it is farther than I thought. So dark. I can not even see my own legs or feet as I walk. I don't know where I am."

"Madam, what is your name?"

"My name?" She sounded worried. "Of course I know my name *perfectly* well. But what is it?"

"Where are you now?"

"I don't know. I don't know!"

"It is alright. Soon you will arrive."

"Yes, at last, a train station."

"Where are you now?"

"On the train."

"Where are you going?"

"To get well."

"Are you sick?"

"I must be. Anyone in so much pain must be sick."

"Do you mean that your leg and knee hurt?"

"I think so, a little, but there is some other pain."

"Where?"

"Nowhere, everywhere, I do not know; I only know I am ill."

"Is it the pain of grief?"

"Perhaps, and fear."

"Where will you go to get well?"

"One goes to Harrogate. Everyone knows that perfectly well."

"How have you paid for the train?"

"Auntie Grannie said, *one always carries money concealed on one's person for emergencies.*"

"Is this an emergency?"

"Indeed yes." She was calm, smiling and settled more comfortably into the chair.

"You seem calm and comfortable now."

"Oh yes. Haven't you ever noticed, everyone is anonymous on a train? I can be silent even among a group of people without it seeming odd, or I can speak at great length to anyone without offering my name."

"So on the train, you do not have to know your own name."

She was delighted. "Correct." Then she grew concerned. "But for all that, I do think it odd that no one notices I am ill or that my stocking is torn and that indeed there is a trace of blood on my skirt hem. Maybe I have disappeared."

"You have not disappeared. They are calling, *All out for Harrogate Yorkshire.* You have arrived at the Hydropathic Hotel. The desk clerk must have your name for the registration book. He is asking, *what is your name, Madam?*"

"A name; some name. I tell the clerk, *Mrs. Theresa Neele.* I tell the clerk at the front desk of the the Hydropathic, *Capetown, Cape of Good Hope.* The clerk asks, *South Africa?* I say, *Yes.*"

"You are Agatha Clarissa Miller Christie. Why did you say Mrs. Neele?"

111

"*Nancy* Neele is Archie's mistress. Archie means for her to be the second Mrs. Archibald Christie."

"If you are now Neele, you will remain Mrs. Archibald Christie?"

"Until death do us part."

"Who is Theresa?"

"A childhood friend that Archie never met. You can not marry someone you have never met. None of this would have happened if I had never met Archie."

"I understand. Your wish, Good Hope, was either to remain Mrs. Christie or never to have met Archie, never been Mrs. Christie. What you do not want is to be in your present situation."

"Yes. It is best and safest to be Mrs. Theresa Neele of South Africa. Africa, so far away, Archie can never meet me."

"You are far away from all trouble. When I count to three, you will wake. You will wake refreshed. You will remember all you have said, but everything you have told me will be very remote. The memory is not in front of you, waiting to be claimed, it is behind you, a harmless memory. One, two, three."

The first thing she said was, "Your list of questions all nicely answered?"

"Let's see. Monty smiling; check. What you did not tell your mother about the dream; check. The meaning of disappearance; check. Why you were angry at Madge; check. Table at Ashfield; check. The nature of The Gun Man and why the nightmares stopped; check."

"You skipped over the reason I spoke of the events in

1926 as if they were *ahead* of me although they were twenty years ago?"

"Good memory." We both smiled.

"Well, why did the past seem to me to be part of my future?"

"Oh, that. Well, remembering it *was* in the future, because you had amnesia, of course."

"Just as I told you."

"Just as you told everyone."

Her voice was gentle and she seemed almost shy. "I left Sunningdale knowing who I was and where I was going. Somewhere on the road to Guilford Station, I lost my memory." She grew excited. "I remember that now. Perfectly."

"Yes, you became lost on that road physically and psychologically."

"It has a certain symmetry."

"When you were hypnotized, there was a point when you knew who you were and what you were doing. You left you car and belongings behind purposefully. You left them because they could identify you as Agatha Christie. Obviously, you knew who you were, why you were leaving, why you were leaving your belongings. You did not want anyone to know where you were going. You wanted to disappear. The road was dark and lonely. It was cold, you were tired, upset . . ."

"Sadness, fatigue, and isolation, like when I forgot my name at Ashfield. So, did I go into a fugue state on the road?"

"No. This time you were physically lost as well, but a fugue state is not the answer."

"Yes, physically lost. I thought, somehow I had thought that Newland Corners was very near Guilford Station."

"You were wrong."

"Wrong."

"Yes, wrong. Guilford was much farther. You were wrong about something you should have been right about."

"Silly of me. I had to pass it to leave the motor. I might have known how far back it was."

"It was more than simply silly; it was symbolic. You had been wrong about more important things that you thought you should be right about."

"The character of my husband. Archie, taking away my . . . what?"

"Your name . . ."

"And giving it to Nancy Neele."

"Your life."

"My *way* of life." She corrected me and rushed on as if fearing I would interrupt. "Can't you tell me now what the clues were that made you sure I knew who I was when I left home?"

"The first is simple; you packed. In a fugue state, one does literally wander off without preparation. You wrote notes. You wrote Campbell Christie: *going to a spa in Yorkshire*. Then what did you do? You went to a spa in Yorkshire."

"The glass mask."

"Absolutely. In the letter you tell Campbell Christie where you are going and, then, dear lady, you go there.

How is it your fault if the world at large searches for you everywhere *else*?"

"Not my fault."

"The champion deceiver, Agatha Christie, is not deceitful. In the spirit of fair play, you lay it all out, and can not be responsible if people did not follow the simple, clear, explicit clues. You follow the rule of your genre: *all clues in plain sight.*"

"Yes, in my books, I make it all perfectly plain, and yet the readers claim they are mystified. If the police had thought a bit instead of rummaging in the underbrush, they could have walked right up to me. I wonder if they mystify themselves."

"You underestimate yourself. Perhaps the police, like your readers, did not quite see the meaning. It's in the wording."

"The wording?"

"Yes, a spa in Yorkshire instead of the Hydropathic Hotel in Harrogate."

"Much the same thing, isn't it? Hydropathic means cure by water, and spa is a place of healing waters."

"Yes, for a wordsmith, exactly the same, but not for everyone. Evidently not for the police."

"Wording?"

"Wording, words, communicating. Your stock and trade, used to illuminate and obscure. What is it the doctor says in *Roger Ackroyd, I left him then.* By the way, it isn't always the least likely suspect."

"No reason why it should be." She had the good grace not to look me in the eye. "It is a preconception the readers bring, a way they mystify themselves."

"Your readers and your doctor," I paused, "and my patient. Won't you ask why I pick psychogenic amnesia over fugue as a diagnosis?"

"Not yet."

"So be it. In your books, and your life, you help with misdirection."

"Do I?"

"The note to Miss Fisher asked that she *cancel* the reservation in Yorkshire."

"I needn't have written to Campbell or Miss Fisher in the first place. I was aboveboard."

"My point exactly. You of all people know that false clues are more confounding than no clues. The letters to Campbell and Miss Fisher were misdirection. It was more than word games. You wrote the notes at the same time. Isn't it logical, though, for the police to assume you wrote Campbell *first* when you had the reservation, and then *later*, asked Miss Fisher to cancel it? Be fair. Doesn't it seem logical for them to conclude you had changed your mind about spas in Yorkshire and were going somewhere else? It is logical, and the police would look everywhere *but* a Yorkshire spa. If they accept the logical and stop thinking, it is not your fault. You hid in plain sight."

"Not my fault."

"If I, the Yank, the neophyte, accept you were weakened by loss of your mother, and you had a warning; there was the threat of divorce, and you had a hallucination; finally there was the certainty of divorce and the fugue state; why it's more than logical, it's *textbook*. If I accepted that, I would stop thinking. But you warned me, take all the clues together. Taken together, the letters, the packed bag, the abandoned car and coat, it was clear you were *running*, not wandering off in fugue."

I was excited at the progress. We were close now; almost through to the other side of the fog. She detoured once more.

"At Harrogate, I gave a name that combined two people to whom this could not be happening. Someone Archie never knew, and someone he loved and *wanted* to marry. Two people who would not have to face the heaping on of shame: divorce and public scandal. I ran away to avoid that."

The excitement died. I could only say, "No."

She ignored my ejaculation as she had ignored whatever I said during the session that she was not ready to face.

"Not very effective was I? By running away I precipitated the public scandal."

My patient was veering off. I did not know how to steer her back, and responded automatically. "The definition of a self-fulfilling prophecy."

"So the decision I made, in full possession of my faculties, was to leave my home."

Her tone was of one tidying up. Everything in its place; time to go. I had believed we were peeling away the layers of confusion and exposing the truth, but evidently there was just so far my patient was willing to go. I determined to try again.

"When you first came into this office, you said that in order to overcome feelings of self-reproach you had to know what happened during the eleven days. You may have done something about which you *should* feel guilty.

117

Knowing, remembering, was the only *cure*. Yet everything you did, every step you took in those eleven days was documented in newsprint. Millions read about it. The abandoned car; the road to Guilford Station, train to London and then to Harrogate; your stay at the Hydro. What you ate for breakfast, when you made a purchase, if you wrote an ad for the newspaper; all discovered and reported. It may not be the same as actual memory, but your actions could *not* have been more ordinary. There was nothing you did about which you, or anyone, could reproach oneself. So whatever it was that you feared would shame you happened *before* you left Sunningdale."

"Obviously I felt guilty about deserting my home, and I hid that from everyone by allowing them to believe I had lost my memory before I left the house."

"Yes."

"I left for the very good reason that I wanted to run away from the shame of divorce."

"No! What made you run?"

"Divorce; public scandal."

"As you sit here today, you have survived both and your book sales soared into the bargain. Agatha, what made you run?"

"But as I have said, I could not have known in advance what effect my actions would have. I *thought* I would avoid shame and loss."

"You said you feared I would stop searching for the truth. It is not I. What made you run? What you could not remember never found its way into the news accounts. Either you were the only witness to the event or it happened inside your own mind . . ."

118

I had found the key.

She said, "Yes." Simply that.

"You did not know which, did you?"

"No. Did I witness something from which I *must* run to save myself, or was it madness, loss of perspective?"

"Let us, together, answer your question. What happened?"

"From the day I *saw* Archie change into The Gun Man at that same table as in my childhood nightmare, I feared I was slowly losing my way; my mind was giving way."

"Stop. Just before you left your home, you wrote those letters and in order to do that, you had to know who you were, and you had to have *planned* to leave home. The letters make that clear. You are responsible for leaving, deserting your home. You left on purpose. You feared you had some reason for feeling guilty; something you had done, then forgotten, about which you should feel guilty; leaving *was* that thing."

"Archie was threatening to leave *me;* how could my leaving be sensible or constructive?"

"You have a strong sense of duty, of family, and you love home, both the concept and houses. You knew you had deserted. It is possible you felt guilty, but I am convinced you had a sound and compelling reason to leave. That reason is the cause of your psychogenic amnesia. It is the cause of all your problems."

"Problems? Don't you mean insanity?"

"Amnesia is not insanity; not in a courtroom, or this room, or any other room. Earlier you said it was illogical for the press to speculate that you ran to cause Archie to come after you. The combination of all the things you did

119

was to assure Archie could not come after you, could not find you. Isn't that it?"

"Misdirection and covering my tracks?"

"Yes, indeed. On the road you suffered from genuine loss of memory. It ought to have been upsetting. Yet, on the train, you did not feel afraid of not knowing who you were."

"I *embraced* not knowing."

"Yes. At Styles, before you left, you believed safety was in no one knowing *where* you were. On the train, you determined safety lay in no one knowing *who* you were. At the Hydro, it was reported that you behaved 'normally.' You were calm, at times, 'gay.' You danced, played games, ate well. What accounts for your mood?"

"You are the doctor."

"It was safest of all not to be you. Say it, Agatha: you were in danger. All your actions are consistent with fleeing from danger; what was the danger? Say it."

"I can't."

"Who did you mistake Archie for when you saw him in the lobby of the Hydro?" I waited. "For heaven's sake I know, but the important thing is that you know. Say it."

"When I saw Archie for the first time in the lobby, he said, *Don't you know me?* I did not. I was frightened and pulled away. He said, *Surely you know me.* He said it in a tone that made me feel so foolish, I tried to guess who he was. *Are you my brother, Monty?* I asked."

"Why did you think he was Monty?"

"Well, they were the only two people I had *seen* as The Gun Man."

120

"When pressed to answer, you supposed Archie was one or the other of your two Gun Men."

"It sounds perfectly horrid to say my husband, my brother were evil Gun Men."

"Exactly, exactly why you could never say it."

I was about to ask the next question to lead her step by step to the end when she said, "You have all the answers now. Let's make an end."

"What were you running from? Say it or you are still running."

"I can't."

"Yet you can. You have. You are indeed the champion deceiver; all in plain sight. The answer is in everything you say. Calling Archie Monty. The changes you made in Psalm 55. Words, some people clarify with words; you use them to mystify. You added five words to the psalm: *my husband, my best friend*. As close as you could come in twenty years to a real-life accusation. Psalm 55 is David speaking to Samuel after he has learned that Saul, whom he has loved and trusted, IS TRYING TO KILL HIM. And David says: *I will die one day at Saul's hand, if I do not rise up and leave his land*."

"Oh, stop. I don't want to remember anymore. That is enough."

"If you truly believed that, you would neither have come to this office nor stayed here. You would have accepted the conclusions of Harley Street."

"What do you want? Do you want me to accuse the father of my child, the man I loved and married, of murder?"

"Hardly that. Here you are."

"Then, what?"

"The truth. No more, no less."

"But what is the truth?"

"To gain his way, to accomplish his ends, you believed Archie would kill you. You ran for your life."

"Yes, I did."

"You believed Archie could see only one possibility and would do it."

"Yes, I did."

"You laid a false trail so he could not find you."

"Yes."

"On December 3, 1926, you realized you were not fighting for a way of life but for your very life."

"Yes."

"You lied all these years about forgetting why you left the house on December 3, so no one would, could ask you why you left. Only during the period from somewhere on the road to Guilford Station through your stay at the Hydro did you feel free of danger."

"Yes. How could I tell anyone? It is true I was restrained by my mother's ideas about what could be said. Yet, it was more than that. You said that I could not, today, accuse Archie of murder because I am alive. But in 1926, I would have been accusing him of the intent to kill. Who would take seriously a writer of murder mystery books, if she accused her husband of intending to kill her?"

"I do."

"I was crying and said, *This will kill me.* He said, *That is one way.* It was what Archie said and his tone. I knew. It was not just a matter of not loving me, he didn't care if I lived or died. I believed he would kill me to have his way."

"Congratulations. For the first time, you have remembered the past and spoken of it in the past tense. You are putting it behind you."

"I did, didn't I?" Heartened, she went on. "Then on the road I lost my way, just as you said."

"Why, *then*?" I asked. The end of the string was more illusive than I had thought. The worst was over. The belief that Archie would murder her in order to marry Nancy Neele was the most deeply buried of her secrets. I knew what she forgot and why she forgot. Yet, I still did not know what explained *when* she forgot.

I was thinking out loud. "Surely the fear was greater standing with Archie at Styles seeing that he could kill you, watch you die, and not feel it, than on the road to Guilford. In fact, the fear of Archie would *lessen* as you got farther away."

"The fear of Archie, perhaps, but not of myself. The farther away I got along that dark, awful road, the more I doubted myself. I was in the wrong. Archie does not like unhappiness. If I could have been stronger, gotten over things. People die. Parents die. Other people are able . . ."

"No. Other people suffer just as you did when a parent dies."

"That, possibly, but I should never have left Archie alone in the city. I should have been at his side."

"Well, that's alright then. If you were there on the lookout, standing guard over him, Archie would have behaved."

"You may be as sarcastic as you like, but losing one's husband to another woman is somehow one's own fault."

"I understand perfectly. Archie did not love you because you were not lovable."

"You are making fun of me."

"A little. You blamed yourself for whatever Archie was and did. You were the betrayed and the betrayer; the victim and the culprit because of what you did do, did not do, or both. You were in the wrong. Almost as proof, you found you were even wrong about simple things like where Guilford Station was."

"The more I blamed myself for Archie's affair, the more clearly I knew Archie could not, would not, murder me. In the room with Archie, I knew he would kill me to have his way. Alone on that dark road, away from Archie, it was ludicrous. Fantasy. The ravings of a deranged mind, and I had acted, not in rational self-protection, but upon such ravings. I was mad, and I was evil. There was no Gun Man, only me, the insane person who *saw* The Gun Man. There was no murderer, only the mind, *my* mind, that created a murderer. My imaginings are the only *real* evil."

"But you did not turn back, go home."

"No. I had refused to give Archie a divorce, and he meant to be rid of me one way or another. I believed my *physical* safety was at risk if I did not give Archie his way. On the dark road I believed my *mental* safety was at risk if I continued to believe my husband was capable of murder. I believed *both* equally. The longer that dark walk, without reference, without being able to *see my way* physically or mentally, the more nightmarish it became."

"And there was no exit."

"I had to give in to Archie or hide from him in order to survive, or, I had to face that I was mad. Either way, it was better not to be me. I had to know, was I mad or he evil; but I hadn't the courage to know."

"Perhaps it was unfortunate that you equated it with the experience with Monty. A silly experience, didn't you say? Of course he would not feed you to the fishes, but you believed it at the time because you were so young. On that long road you may have wondered if it was the same with your perception of Archie. Yet there was no way to know for sure. The fear of Archie was equal to the condemnation of yourself."

"Yes. I lost my memory when the only two ideas I had in my head were: my husband plans to murder me, and I am mad for thinking such a thing. I could have borne either thought. I could not bear not knowing which was true. I had to get right away from myself. And I did . . . somehow."

"The fear that Archie might kill you was one with which you could cope; did cope. You made a plan; set a false trail; protected yourself. On the road, you lost your way. To know you are in danger is one thing, to be unsure is intolerable because it prevents you from protecting yourself. It makes you *more* vulnerable to danger."

"Safety lay in not being me. What followed was a feeling of great relief from the struggle of trying to determine what was the truth. There was also a feeling of safety." She paused and exhaled. "So there it all is, the whole sordid story. No one would have believed me then. Even now, *you* do not believe Archie could have murdered me, do you?"

"Archie is not my concern; you are."

"I will never know which it was, my madness or Archie's."

"We will never know what he intended, and it doesn't matter."

"*Doesn't* matter? What could matter more?"

"You could matter more. Knowing you were never crazy could matter more. If he planned to murder you or not, you believed, *with good cause*, that Archie might go to the extreme of murder to get what he wanted."

"Good cause?"

"Good cause. How many times has Poirot described the psychology of the murderer? The selfish person who only values his own desires? You understand perfectly that you had good cause for your fears."

"Good cause."

"It was intuition, not madness; perception, not illness, that led you to recognize danger. You were undoubtedly weakened, ill if you like, by grief and sadness and anger. But still you could see and understand the people around you and do something constructive. What is the course of action when you discover you are married to someone who did not marry you for better and for worse, in sickness and in health? Someone who cared for himself to the absolute exclusion of others? You saw him for what he was, that was sufficient cause to run. It seems quite rational to me."

"I had *good* cause. By December, I saw the selfishness, the blind will to be with Nancy Neele without concern for anything else. I saw the lack of any caring left for me. My vain hope that he would change his mind had prompted my refusal to grant a divorce voluntarily. Now I saw that my refusal to do as he wished could drive him to violence."

"Unfortunately that reminded you of trailing after Monty. It is easy to see how you would equate one with the other. You were trailing after Archie when he wanted you to go away. However, making that connection compounded the problem. The comparison confused you because you had determined that in the case of Monty your perception had been inaccurate, childish. It is bad enough to have to protect yourself physically from your own husband, but not being sure if the threat is real was, for you, sheer horror. I only see you did a very clever thing in December 1926: constructive, adequate, and sufficient to meet the problem."

"*That* is what you see?"

"It is."

She was eager and interested. It was an important moment. She had coped with her shame, fear, and confusion about past events by forgetting them. To aid her in remembering carried a responsibility with it: allow the memory and dispel the shame, fear, and confusion.

I began. "You got safely away from potential danger without accusing your daughter's father with threatening that danger. Neat. You assured your survival without any accusation or explanation. You avoided legal charges, courts, burdens of proof that, in the process, would destroy both of you whatever the verdict. As an added bonus, without leveling a single charge, when next you had to face Archie, it was under the watchful eye of a policeman who brought him to identify you. In fact, by then the whole world was watching and the accusation had been made by eager newshounds and not by you. You had assured your safety, and given yourself what you needed. Time. Congratulations, Mrs. Mallowan."

"And I acted with good cause. It was perception not madness."

I nodded. "Whether he had planned ever to raise a finger against you, he had already been willing to watch you suffering, ill and in pain, and not *lift* a finger to help."

"I was right to act as I did."

"Archie and the gas leak. You were right in both cases. An embarrassment of riches."

"How odd for you to say that. It was the gas leak that brought me here. Gave me, after all those years, the courage to try and reclaim the lost days."

"Really, the gas leak?"

"Yes. You see it was almost a small reenactment of those days in 1926. Then and with the gas leak, no one shared my perception. They actually thought me mad, however much they treated me with sympathy and condescension. I pressed on, and I was right about the open gas pipe. I prevailed and so I decided, it was the time. I was ready to face 1926." She paused. "All these years I was tormented because I believed I had to *know*. Yet what I believed I had to know was too frightening to remember. If Archie meant to kill me for denying him a divorce, then he was evil. If I had thought that was his intent but it was not, then I was mad. The consequence of knowing, in either case, was devastating. Now I see that I did not have to know. I acted to protect myself with good cause and without harming anyone else."

"Like moving out of the path of a hurricane. Whether

it makes landfall or not, it was prudent to get out of the way."

"As a result, everyone survived."

"Congratulations, again."

She extended her hand. "This time I *am* leaving." We shook hands. "Thank you. You have given me back my memory and my self-respect. What can I give you in return?"

"More than you already have?"

"I?"

"Yes, in my field we are convinced all actions are motivated from within. We seem to have forgotten people live in the world among other people. Your experience was motivated by outside events. It is an important lesson you taught me. You have shown me why often I have felt uncomfortable in my field. You are my first patient, and because of that and what I learned from you, I am comfortable for the first time in my professional role."

"Throw away the textbooks?"

"If I can find them," I pulled at my ear and looked vaguely around my office, "now that you have tidied up."

"But, seriously, what is your fee?"

"Shall I make it twenty-five pounds? For symmetry?"

"Perfect," she said reaching for her purse.

"No," I said. "Not enough."

"Not?" She paused. "I know. I shall give you this story since it was mine, but remembering it is ours. You must promise, however, not to tell it until I am dead and gone."

"Oh, dear lady. I wanted . . . only wanted to be able

129

to say I was hugged by the incomparable Agatha Christie on a rainy day in London."

"Easily done."

We hugged and she took her leave.

Epilogue

The room is quiet, perhaps expectant.

The Analyst says, "I may have been, continued to be, unconventional in some of my methods, but the manner of my diagnosis was conventional. It was arrived at by the process of elimination. I recommend it. You will generally be faced with multiple symptoms. In the rare case, the diagnosis will be obvious, the symptoms will fit only one interpretation. Generally, symptoms will be consistent with more than one disease or disorder.

"I first asked myself, was the amnesia genuine? Once I was satisfied that here was a genuine case of amnesia, I eliminated chemically induced amnesia and amnesia due to physical trauma. I then considered fugue state or psychogenic amnesia. Once I had eliminated fugue state because her leaving home was planful not a wandering away, I was left with psychogenic amnesia. A necessary prerequisite to the onset of psychogenic amnesia is fear for one's life. I knew then that I was looking for a threat, real or imagined, to her life."

The room is so quiet that when one student in the audience says to the person sitting next to her, "I think he meant to kill her," everyone hears the words.

The room instantly divides into two camps. A student on the opposing side reacts. "Bunk."

She responds defensively, "The callousness of the man. He was psychologically capable of anything."

"Ridiculous. So he wanted a divorce; divorce her. What could be simpler?"

The Analyst clears his throat. "Today, perhaps. But in 1926 in England, divorce was difficult. The petitioner needed grounds. Archie did not have grounds; hard to be both the adulterer and the petitioner."

There is general mumbled disbelief.

"Quite true," the Analyst says. "He needed Agatha to file for the divorce."

The student, so certain of his position, wavers. "That makes a difference. To get what he wanted, he needed Agatha Christie to do something . . ."

"That she would not do." This interruption is from the other camp and is said with satisfaction.

"Oh, lord. Motive." Those in Colonel Christie's camp groan.

Those who believe Archie meant to kill Agatha take heart and chime in, "Professor, you should have *told* her."

"What?" the Analyst asks.

"The facts." They speak as one.

"Assume I know the facts . . ." the Analyst begins.

"Absolutely. You do." Another student interrupts. "Archie's neglect at a time when she needed him was tantamount to abuse. Archie Christie showed himself capable of any selfish act, even the most selfish act, murder."

"That is not fact, it is theory." The other camp remains strident.

"The fact is Archie *didn't* harm her, and that is the

best predictor that he would not have. He just stayed out of her way; how is that abuse?"

"Well, well," the Analyst intercedes, "it is relevant to point out to both sides that what we professionals do the *least* adequately is predict human behavior. Remember Dame Agatha cited Dr. Bateson at one point. He said that if you kick a rock and know the size of the rock, the direction in which you kicked it, and the energy with which you kicked it, you can predict the rock will leave the ground and even where it will land. If you kick a man, knowing all the same data," the Analyst spreads his hands in surrender, "you still can predict nothing about what the man will do."

"You are right, Professor. You can not predict Archie would harm her based on what he did to that date, December 1926. Colonel Christie had no obligation to his wife when she was suffering. Other people don't make you sick and can't make you well."

The Analyst is troubled. "My goodness, if that is true, what are we doing at this school? In fact, why this school at all? If we are powerless to help, what is the point of our studies, our field?"

Another student, equally sure of what is right, says, "Your patient needed more that you gave her. She needed the comfort of knowing her assumption was true. Her life was truly in danger. Colonel Christie could not marry Nancy Neele without a divorce or Agatha Christie's death; he could not live with her the way people do today without benefit of marriage; he could not persuade Agatha to divorce him, and *he wanted to be with Nancy.*"

"So, assume we *know* that, how would it profit my

patient? My patient was Agatha Christie, not Archie. Her life was not with him, but away from him. What she needed to know was that her behavior was rational and constructive and that she had nothing in her past that should frighten or shame her. That is the assurance she took away."

There is silence on both sides.

The Analyst asks, "Tell me this, what could she have done if she had known, that she did not do with only suspicion?"

Still both sides are silent.

"She had the strength and courage to protect herself, to act on her convictions, without absolute proof, and to do so without harm to others."

One student stands up. "She might have suffered less if she had been sure."

"No, she might have suffered less if she could have completely accepted her own opinions. She suffered when she doubted. She would have suffered more with proof."

"More?"

"Well, what form could proof take? A witnessed attack on her person? A successful homicide?"

A heretofore silent student groans, "So we began by not knowing about one thing, and end by not knowing another. We solved the mystery of the lost days of Agatha Christie and are left with the mystery of the character of Archie Christie."

"Isn't it grand?" the Analyst enthuses.

The audience groans.

"You fail to recognize that Agatha Christie did not want to know if Archie had murder in his heart. Nor did she wish to die. Do not fail your patient. Ultimately you are there to serve the patient not yourself."

"But not knowing. Isn't the point of any science, every profession really, to find everything out?"

"Listen. *The persistent effort of so-called modern minds to explain mysteries . . . can yield nothing, in the long run, but the nostalgic satisfaction of the small boy who discovers at last that his mechanical duck was made up of two wheels, three springs, and a screw, objects which are doubtless reassuring, but he has lost his mechanical duck, and he has usually not found an explanation [as to how it works].* That is Jean Anouilh. Learn it by heart before you enter your professional offices. Don't be in a hurry to take your patients apart. Knowing isn't helping. Know enough to help and heal; don't probe to take apart and destroy. If you want to know all the facts, become a lawyer. If you only care what makes things tick, become an engineer. If all you want is facts and answers, stay in the laboratory, dissect behavior and give lectures to your colleagues, but don't add to the burden of the sufferers who look to you for relief. There are things of value in this world that are not hard edged, clean cut, neat, and absolute.

"In Agatha Christie's books intuition stands with fact; ethics and morals are equal to law. She creates a world in which we all live comfortably because it is expected, recognized, and another amorphous thing, nice. That is why we revisit her even after we know who-done-it. Leave it that we have solved one mystery about Agatha Christie yet there will always be mysteries about others, even about ourselves. Isn't that grand?"

137

Dr. Owens received her doctorate from Yeshiva University in 1987. She is a Licensed Independent Clinical Social Worker and Licensed Marriage and Family Therapist in the state of Massachusetts as well as a Licensed Clinical Social Worker in the state of Maryland. She is a Clinical Member of the American Association of Marriage and Family Therapists, a Certified Member of the American Association of Clinical Mental Health Counselors, and a member of the New York Academy of Sciences. Her doctoral dissertation, *Clinical v. Psychometric Judgement,* is a study of comparative methods of diagnosis. Other books by the author are *The Berkshire Cottages: A Vanishing Era; Bellefontaine; FundRaising,* editor; *The Stockbridge Story,* contributor.